# Samsung 3.0

## TALENT, TECHNOLOGY AND TIMING

Eun Y. Kim, Ph.D.
with Edward C. Valdez

*88 Things You Need
to Know about Samsung*

CEO International
*CEOINTL@aol.com*
*drkimglobal@gmail.com*
www.drkimglobal.com

Cover Design © 2013 Edward C. Valdez

Samsung 3.0: Talent, Technology and Timing/ Eun Y. Kim with Edward C. Valdez —2nd edition

ISBN 978-1-886291-02-7

# Contents

Preface.................................................................................................................vii

How to Read This Book.....................................................................................xi

Section 1: Samsung's Story and History...........................................................1

   1. A Humble Beginning with Three Criteria ....................................................3

   2. Built to Last for 300 Years ........................................................................6

   3. Competition Makes You Stronger ...............................................................8

   4. Predestined for Success with a Name........................................................10

   5. 1993—Change Everything Except Your Wife and Children......................12

   6. 1996—Design or Resign ...........................................................................15

   7. 1997—Transform Dangers into Opportunities.........................................17

   8. 2003—Discover Three Geniuses and China ...............................................19

   9. 2013—Be More Paranoid at the Top.........................................................21

   10. 2020—Inspire the World, Create the Future ..........................................23

Section 2: Founder's Legacy—The Midas Hands of Byung-Chull Lee.............25

   11. Read the Times for the Right Timing ......................................................27

   12. Be Preoccupied with Two Questions.......................................................29

   13. Benchmark Japan ....................................................................................31

   14. Tap All Bridges Before Crossing.............................................................33

   15. It Is I Who Give Orders ...........................................................................35

   16. Delegate Only If You Trust .....................................................................37

   17. Spend 80% of Your Time Developing Talent...........................................39

   18. Listen with Respect .................................................................................41

   19. Only the Best-in-Class Will Survive .......................................................43

   20. Merit First, Even for Family Succession Planning...................................45

Section 3: Kun-Hee Lee: The CEO Nobody Knows .........................................47

   21. Greater than Jack Welch? ........................................................................49

   22. The Most Important Subject of My Study Is People..................................51

   23. Like Father, Like Son: Reading the Times...............................................53

   24. Think 3D..................................................................................................55

25. Benchmark Small, but Strong Countries ........................................ 57

26. Lead like Ben-Hur .................................................................... 59

27. Apply the Lessons from Golf, Rugby and Baseball ................... 61

28. It's a Crime to Manufacture Products with Defects ................... 63

29. Master the Art of Communication ............................................ 65

30. Pave the Road for Successors ................................................... 67

Section 4: The Samsung Empire ...................................................... 69

31. The Republic or Kingdom of Samsung? ................................... 71

32. Balance of Executive Power and Influence ............................... 73

33. Images of Samsung and "Samsung Men" ................................ 75

34. Samsung Citizen's Life: From Cradle to Grave ........................ 78

35. Pledge of Allegiance: Company First! ..................................... 80

36. Samsung Constitution .............................................................. 83

37. Do You Speak Samsung? .......................................................... 85

38. Cluster Samsung Towns for Efficiency and Synergy ................ 87

39. Border Control and Security Solutions ..................................... 89

40. Document and Share to Triple Sales ......................................... 91

Section 5: Samsung Inside ................................................................ 93

41. Korean Culture vs. Samsung Culture ........................................ 95

42. Fusion Leadership—East Meets West ...................................... 97

43. Perpetual Crisis and Contingency Plan .................................... 99

44. Work Week—Mon., Tues., Wed., Thurs., Fri., Fri. and Fri. ...... 101

45. Samsung Speed—Survival of the Fastest ................................. 103

46. Fight like a Pit Bull ................................................................. 105

47. It's No Longer the Old Samsung .............................................. 107

48. Everyone Deserves an MBA ..................................................... 109

49. Ethics and Integrity ................................................................. 111

50. Etiquette Is Competitiveness ................................................... 113

Section 6: Talent = Company ............................................................ 115

51. Search the Globe for Three Geniuses ....................................... 117

52. Discover Tech and Design Talent ............................................. 119

53. "SPEC" and Stories of New Hires ........................................... 121

54. Samsung Talent "Military" Academy ....................................... 123

55. Invest in Building Glocal Experts ............................................ 125

56. Lee Daughters and the Rise of Samsung Women ................................... 127

57. Leadership Wisdom from Asian Sages..................................... 130

58. Nurture Your Career like an Orchid ......................................... 132

59. Samsung Pipeline for Korean Leaders ....................................... 134

60. The CEO Is a Global Headhunter.............................................. 136

Section 7: Sales, Marketing and PR............................................... 139

61. Know Your Competition ....................................................... 141

62. Move Customers to Tears..................................................... 143

63. D'Light Customers with Quality.............................................. 145

64. Product with a Soul ............................................................. 147

65. Premium Brand Power ......................................................... 149

66. Topping Coca-Cola in Advertising........................................... 151

67. Samsung Everywhere with Sports Marketing.............................. 153

68. The Cheapest Way to Influence Opinion Leaders ........................ 155

69. Even a Lawsuit Can Be Good Publicity..................................... 157

70. Smart Social Media ............................................................. 159

Section 8: For Partners, Suppliers and Global Employees ................... 161

71. Know *Kap-Eul* (Customer-Supplier) Dynamics ........................ 163

72. Build Relationships, but Be Aware........................................... 165

73. Do Due Diligence for Negotiation ........................................... 167

74. Soften Your Energy and Save Face .......................................... 169

75. Don't Try to Educate Customers ............................................. 171

76. The Art of Cross-Cultural Communication ................................ 173

77. Read *Nunchi* and Expect *Kimchi*....................................... 175

78. Share Only What You Are Willing to Lose ................................ 177

79. Connect with the Human Side of Koreans ................................. 179

Section 9: Feedforward to Samsung: Suggestions for the Future...................... 181

80. Innovate Smart with a Soul ................................................... 183

81. Overcome the NIH (Not Invented Here) Syndrome ..................... 186

82. Upgrade Leadership with a Global Mindset................................ 188

83. Try Harder to Retain Global Talent.......................................... 191

84. Work Smart, Play Smart ....................................................... 194

85. Loosen Control.................................................................. 197

86. Pursue Co-Prosperity with Partners ......................................... 199

87. Do the Right Thing.................................................................202

88. Inspire the World with Humility and Grace.............................205

Epilogue.....................................................................................207

Acknowledgements....................................................................210

Bibliography..............................................................................211

# Preface

Almost 25 years ago when I read *Made in Japan: Akio Morita and Sony*, I dreamed of the day that I would write a book entitled *Made in Korea*. Korea just successfully hosted the 1988 Seoul Olympics. Koreans were excited about showing off the "Miracle on the Han River" built on the ashes of the Korean War (1950-1953). Korea was on the threshold of transition from a developing country to a developed nation. But I wasn't sure whether such a book would be possible in my lifetime. In Korea, I grew up hearing that Japan was at least 50 years ahead of Korea in education, technology and its political system. Some Koreans believed that the rumor had been spread by those Japanese who wanted to create an inferiority complex in the minds of Koreans; nonetheless, many Koreans seemed to accept that it would take a long time to catch up to Japan, which had colonized Korea between 1910 and 1945.

When I was in graduate school in the 1980s, *Japan As No. 1: Lessons for America* by Ezra Vogel was popular reading for academics and businessmen in the United States. Professors from B-Schools to Public Affairs Schools touted Japanese supremacy in education, manufacturing and management practices. Japan did almost everything right. US Corporations offered three-to-five-day classes on "Doing Business with Japan." From long school hours to Just-In-Time manufacturing and life-long employment, Japan was Number One.

Then Japan suffered from a serious recession in the 1990s. Soon the world's interest in Japanese management practices tapered off and the four tigers of Asia—Korea, Hong Kong, Taiwan and Singapore—got more attention.

Interestingly, Korea was the only country without the Chinese language and heritage. By the year 2000, the rapid growth of China and India became the focus of the business world's interest. But at the same time, two Korean companies started flexing their muscles and gaining prestige across the globe: Samsung and Hyundai.

I have been privileged to work with both companies. In 1981, I was one of the first college graduate women professionals hired by a Korean conglomerate. Hyundai was a pioneer in recruiting women and I joined the international business department at Hyundai Construction that had multiple projects in the Middle East. At the time, Samsung, like many other Korean conglomerates, didn't hire women for professional positions.

Fortunately, I have had numerous opportunities to work with various entities of Samsung, from semiconductors to telecommunications, and their partners for over 20 years, and have become an accidental life-long student and follower of Samsung. As a global leadership coach and cross-cultural management consultant, I have watched the group rise from an unknown original equipment manufacturer (OEM) company to be among the Top 10 Global Brands. As Samsung improved its global game and introduced the "Samsung Way" to its worldwide operations, I wondered whether the Samsung Way could be benchmarked in a broader and more systematic fashion like the GE Way and the Toyota Way.

The unique Korean cultural and political context coupled with Samsung's strong owner-control management techniques planted some doubts. How many global companies are run by a powerful owner-leader who is willing to bet his fortune to implement his vision? Most professional managers wouldn't have the luxury of investing in super-scale projects and rolling out "shock therapy" change management initiatives, which Samsung founder Byung-Chull Lee and his son and successor Kun-Hee Lee did. Politically, starting from the 1960s, the Korean government kept its pro-business environment to enable export-led growth, granting Korean conglomerates like Samsung special finance and tax policies.

Samsung has certainly not been built by the Lee family alone. Samsung is a product of talent, technology and timing based on the owners' vision and control. They have had the magic of turning ordinary talent into extraordinary talent with their investment in people and technology.

I have heard the good, the bad and the ugly of Samsung from people who worked at or with Samsung's global operations. Companies are made of people. Granted that we are all fallible and no one is perfect, Samsung is a company far from perfection. This book is mainly about the good, because my goal is to share Samsung's best practices with people and companies across the globe. Cultural values are often the ideals and have the best intentions. So Samsung's corporate culture and values described in this book can be the ideals. This book is also mostly about the practices of Samsung Electronics (SEC) Korea, not those of all of the Samsung Group with more than 70 entities or those of SEC's global subsidiaries. Although there are some core values that Samsung group companies share based on the founder's business philosophy, SEC shines in its operation, contributing to almost 70% of the group's annual sales.

This book covers in detail the unique global leadership practices rooted in the Eastern way of thinking. The 20th century leadership and management theories were dominated by Western thinkers. Given that more than half of the world population lives in Asia, the rise of Chindia (China and India) and the potential growth of Southeast Asia, it's time to more seriously consider Eastern leadership principles that have existed for thousands of years.

I hope that this book will inspire leaders, managers and students in developing countries to see that it is possible to rise from adversity. Only 60 years ago, Korea was a country devastated by the Korean War. Even before the war, many African countries such as Ghana, Kenya and Morocco had higher GDPs per capita than Korea. In the early 1960s, there were not enough employment opportunities in Korea because it was one of the poorest countries in the world with less than $100 GDP per capita. Thus, between 1963 and 1977, over 7,900 Korean miners and 11,100 nurses went to what was then West Germany to take the jobs that Germans didn't want. Korean miners, some with higher education, had to collect coal in the underground mine 1,000 meters deep, with temperatures over 40°C (104°F). Young nurses from Korea cleaned corpses at hospitals just because their native country was poor and couldn't provide them with jobs. It has been reported that then President Chung-Hee Park couldn't finish his speech at a gathering of Koreans during his visit to Germany in 1964. He was going to deliver words of encouragement to Korean nurses and miners, but they started crying during the Korean anthem. He set aside his prepared speech and wept with them. "You must be very lonely because you miss home and family. Let's do our best to bring honor to our motherland. We may not achieve it in our lifetime, but let's lay the foundation for prosperity for our descendants," said Mr. Park with tears. There was no single dry eye in the audience.

Samsung's founder had a similar vision to bring Koreans out of poverty. Koreans set education and hard work as their top priorities to achieve prosperity. With visionary leaders and dedicated citizens, anything is possible. If Korea and Samsung could do it, any country and company can do it.

For Samsung's competitors and partners, this book will help them be better prepared for a business war—whether it is a Smartphone War, Memory War, Appliance War or Price War. According to the Chinese sage, Lao-Tzu, "Knowing others is intelligence, knowing self is true wisdom." Another sage, Sun-Tzu, wrote in *The Art of War*, "If you know your enemies and know yourself, you will not be imperiled in a hundred battles." The Samsung Way will show readers the way to a global fusion leadership style that attempts to combine the best of East and West.

For Samsung insiders, I hope this book will provide food for thought in their pursuit of international excellence. The year of 2013 marked the 20th anniversary of Samsung's New Management that had been declared on June 7th, 1993 in Frankfurt, Germany and considered as Samsung's "cultural revolution." Koreans believe that "mountains and rivers will change in 10 years," so Samsung announced New Management 2.0 in 2003. Another 10 years has passed since and the global economic landscape has changed again, yielding mountains with steeper slopes and rivers with more winding paths. So for Samsung, it is time for another upgrade: New Management 3.0.

The Asian philosophy of yin-yang teaches us that everything has two sides. The positives have negatives within them and vice versa. In my earlier book, *The Yin and Yang of American Culture: A Paradox*, I wrote that these complementary opposites have influenced Asians as they seek balance in the universe and in their lives. Yin and yang forces coexist in everything. They complete each other to maintain cosmic harmony and can transform into each other. For example, water, which is yin, changes into ice, which is yang. Furthermore, an entity regarded as yin in one light can be regarded as yang in another light. So in any virtue, there's a potential for vice; in any vice, there's a possibility for virtue. Thus, Samsung's strengths could become weaknesses if they are not managed well. The virtues that got Samsung to the top of the world could turn into vices. Of course, Samsung has the potential to turn its vices into virtues as well.

In his famous Stanford University commencement speech, the late Steve Jobs of Apple advised: "Stay hungry, stay foolish." Samsung is hungrier than ever. Sun-Tzu said, "Speed is the essence of war. Take advantage of the enemy's unpreparedness." With its talent and technology, Samsung can certainly use timing for their advantage. Yet only when Samsung becomes a world-class company with Asian humility and grace, will it become an inspiration for all who strive for global humanity and prosperity.

# How to Read This Book

Korean name starts with the family name first. For example, my name would be written Kim Eun-Young. For this book, it will follow the order of an English name with the surname at the end. Korean newspapers often use the two initials of a given name of political leaders. For example, former President Myung-Bak Lee was frequently called MB, although not in person or in any official document. In corporations too, often the initials are used when employees talk about their leaders. Samsung doesn't use the two initials of its founder and his successor. However, two initials of their first names will be used to address them in this book. Below are the abbreviations of Samsung family members in this book.

- BC: Byung-Chull Lee (1910-1987), Founder
- KH: Kun-Hee Lee (1942-), Current Chairman. BC's third son
- JY (or Jay): Jae-Yong Lee (1968-), Vice Chairman and Heir Apparent, KH's only son.

"Samsung men" used in this book is gender neutral and includes female employees as well.

For e-book readers, you may notice inconsistent spacing depending on your device. We are working to standardize spacing across applications. To better understand the symbolic meanings for Samsung's present and future within the eyes of KH Lee and JY Lee (front and back covers), please zoom-in on the images of their pupils and read Chapter 80.

In *The Art of War*, Sun-Tzu said:

> *"It's not the war between the strong and the weak, but the survival of the fastest... the faster eats the slower. If a war is not speedy, even if one wins the war, the loss will be greater than a win.*
>
> *Speed is the essence of war. Take advantage of the enemy's unpreparedness. Travel by unexpected routes and strike him where he has taken no precautions."*

# I

# Samsung's Story
# and History

## CHAPTER 1

# A Humble Beginning
# with Three Criteria

*"A small businessman thinks about only short-term profits, but a big
businessman explores the ways to enrich everyone."*

— Konosuke Matsushita,
founder of Panasonic

Samsung Group, the largest Korean conglomerate, was founded by Byung-Chull
Lee in 1938 during the Japanese colonization of Korea. "Samsung Sanghoe"
started in Daegu in the Northern Gyungsang Province, as a trading company
dealing with light and small commodities, such as rice, flour, sugar and other farm
goods in contrast to the heavy machinery and big items which Hyundai focused on.
The success of Samsung Sanghoe led to a creation of Samsung Trading Co. in 1948.
The company was very profitable within one and one-half years. However, it quickly
became a victim of the Korean War (1950-1953). BC did not give up, and worked hard
to expand markets and develop products for export. While Samsung made fortunes in
trading, BC reflected on the true spirit of entrepreneurship. He was dissatisfied with
selling imported products, even if the business was extremely profitable. "How long are
we Koreans going to rely on imported products? Shouldn't we be able to produce them
ourselves?" asked BC. That was Samsung's turning point to become a world leader in
manufacturing. He had his team conduct a feasibility study for building a manufacturing facility. Eventually, Samsung diversified itself into areas such as insurance and retail.

According to Samsung's website, Samsung laid the strategic foundations for its
future growth by investing in the heavy, chemical and petrochemical industries in the

1970s. During that time, Samsung also took steps to enhance its global position in the textile industry. It integrated its manufacturing processes from raw materials to end products, creating new companies such as Samsung Heavy Industries, Samsung Shipbuilding and Samsung Precision.

BC had a conviction that those who had technology would rule the world. Instead of doing assembly work for other companies, BC invested in adopting technologies early on. Samsung Electronics, already a major manufacturer in the Korean market, began to export its products for the first time during this period. Samsung solidified its position by acquiring a 50 percent stake in Korea Semiconductor in 1974. After experiencing an "oil shock" in 1973, KH was also convinced that Korea would need value-added high tech industry. In 1978, Samsung Semiconductor and Samsung Electronics became separate entities. Later Samsung added the aerospace business and entered the system development business to be a leader in information technology. The 76 years of Samsung's growth is breathtaking. BC turned a small business into a conglomerate and KH has turned a Korean conglomerate into a global powerhouse.

Samsung means three stars in Chinese characters. BC chose three because it is the favorite number of many Koreans. The number 4 is associated with death, so Koreans avoid the 4th floor and some elevators don't have a 4th floor button. He chose stars to symbolize Samsung's future to be bright, high and forever brilliant. It was a humble beginning, but BC had a burning desire to improve the Korean economy. He was ambitious, but practical. When he entered into a new business, he used clear criteria for decisions:

- What are the needs of our country?
- How would it benefit our fellow Koreans?
  (This later expanded into global citizens.)
- Can we compete in the global market?

BC believed that what was good for Korea was good for Samsung and vice versa. He was compelled to provide Koreans with jobs and necessities to maintain their quality of life after the war. Protecting his country through successful enterprises became his motto. BC's belief became an important part of his successor's management philosophy. KH said,

*"It is a crime for management to make a company go bankrupt and employees lose jobs. Workforce reduction may be the easiest, but the most difficult solution. It is important to prevent layoffs in advance through effective collaboration of management and labor."*

## CHAPTER 2

# Built to Last for
# 300 Years

A university professor who was one of BC's advisors was in a meeting with him and several Samsung Presidents:

*BC: Please study what we need to do if we want the company to last for 300 years.*

*Professor Lee: Is there any reason that you say for 300 years?*

*BC (smiling): I want to say 1,000 or 10,000 years, but if I say that, everyone is going to think that I'm greedy. In other countries, there are 300-year-old companies. I thought that we could benchmark them. And if a company lasted 300 years, it could last 500 years or 1,000 years.*

*Professor Lee: Are you saying that the company will be run by your descendants? Or are you talking about a company that will last for 300 years?*

*BC: It will be great if my children and their children can run it. However, that is impossible. These days, young people don't like to have too many kids. And it's difficult to know whether any one of them will be capable of or fit for running our business. My desire is to see the company Samsung built to last.*

Do great business leaders think alike? Steve Jobs also said, "My passion has been to build an enduring company where people were motivated to make great products. Everything else was secondary." BC and Jobs had something in common. Both wanted their companies to endure a long time. BC's desire for continuity must have been inspired by Japanese enterprises. According to Tokyo Shoko Research, more than 20,000 companies in Japan have been in business for over 100 years. Some are even more than 1,000 years old.

In 2013, Samsung celebrated its 75th anniversary and is dashing to last at least another 25 years with a search for new growth engines. KH has groomed his son JY and daughters to become global leaders who will lead Samsung to become at least a 100 year-old institution. In addition, Samsung has accelerated mergers of different subsidiaries to increase competitiveness through economies of scale. For example, three prongs of Samsung Electronics—consumer electronics, mobile & IT and semiconductors used to be different companies. But when KH became Chairman, he ordered them to be under one entity. In 2014, Samsung SDI and Cheil Industries announced their merger to advance into a "global total energy and materials solution provider." Samsung has been continuously restructuring and reorganizing various entities for operational excellence that will lead to corporate longevity. Considering that even some of Korea's top 30 conglomerates and global giants have disappeared in the last ten years, Samsung is keenly aware that they cannot just rely on their past laurels.

## CHAPTER 3

# Competition Makes You Stronger

When Samsung wanted to start an electronics company in 1969, LG (then Gold Star) was a leader in the domestic TV market. The market was already saturated and the Korean government was concerned that Samsung's entry would hurt small and medium-sized companies in the industry. In addition to unfavorable external conditions, BC faced another dilemma. On the family front, LG and Samsung were related by marriage: BC's second daughter was married to a son of the LG founder—the Koo family. Samsung's interest in an electronics company was a signal of competition with in-laws. Yet, BC was persistent. He met with then-Korean President Jeong-Hee Park (father of the current [first female] President Geun-Hye Park), and successfully persuaded him to approve his new business. Japan's Sanyo Electric Co. became a partner and taught Samsung how to make televisions. And the rest is history.

BC justified that competition in domestic markets would contribute to the success of both LG and Samsung. Samsung would keep LG and other competitors on their toes and prevent them from complacency while helping them innovate faster. He was right. LG and Samsung, competing against each other in the domestic market first, have become the top two global players in electronics. BC's vision might be the reason why two-thirds of mobile phones and TV sets sold in the U.S. are made by LG or Samsung.

LG is no longer the most serious competition for Samsung; however, Samsung cannot seem to accept not being Number One. Samsung has been behind LG in the chemical industry. In early 2014 Samsung announced mergers of six companies into two in the areas related with chemical materials. It is reported that Samsung will attempt to beat LG with competitiveness gained from a larger size.

Competition is created inside Samsung as well. For example, same projects may be given to two different teams or organizations to compete against each other. Such internal competition is not always welcomed; however, they often put competing teams on their toes and bring the best out of them.

## THE CATFISH THEORY

When BC was a young entrepreneur in his 20s, he experimented with raising fish in a farm. He put 1,000 loaches in one pond and the number of loaches grew to 2,000 in a year. So the following year, he put 1,000 loaches in a pond and the other 1,000 into another pond, but with 20 catfishes. After a year, he found 2,000 loaches in the first pond where the loaches were alone. But in the pond with the catfishes, he found 4,000 loaches and 200 catfishes. The loaches moved faster to avoid being eaten by catfishes. And the fish got healthier and the meat was tastier as they moved around. In the universe, living things get stronger through adversity and competition.

## CHAPTER 4

# Predestined for Success
# with a Name

"The End of Samsung." That was the market response when Samsung announced its entry into the semiconductor industry and memory chip business in 1983. "How can Samsung make memory chips even when they can't make good TVs?" Cynics laughed at Samsung. The Mitsubishi Research Institute in Japan cited five reasons for Samsung's failure, including a small domestic market in Korea, a weak related industry, need for indirect capital, Samsung's low technology and its small scale.

The skeptics didn't understand the invincible Korean spirit of *oghi*, which means one's determination to prove that naysayers are wrong. Also, they underestimated BC's perfectionist streak. His decision was made only after comparing vast amounts of research data and doing feasibility studies. He found that the U.S. was more advanced in technology development than Japan, but that Japan was ahead of the U.S. in manufacturing, creating profits from mass production. BC believed that if Japan could do it, Korea could do it.

His third son KH, who was working for BC, was also a strong supporter. In 1974, almost 10 years before Samsung's official announcement of its entry into the memory business, KH had acquired 50% of an almost bankrupt semiconductor company called Korea Semiconductor for half a million dollars. Faced with Samsung executives' opposition, KH offered to use his own money for the acquisition. He countered every objection and cynic with possibility thinking. He saw the importance of the semiconductor business for the 21st century innovation and called memory chips the rice (staple) of the industry. Business is all about timing. KH believed that the timing was perfect for Samsung to move quickly into semiconductors. He explained why Korea is perfect for the semiconductor business: It requires dexterity, precision, and cleanliness:

- Koreans are dexterous, thanks to using chopsticks.
- Koreans are very hygiene-oriented, thanks to the indoor slippers they use.
- Koreans are team-oriented due to communal dining.

Soon after the announcement, Samsung sent its smartest engineers to Micron Technology, Inc. in the U.S., a new business partner in Samsung's move into the semi-conductor field. Samsung had signed an agreement with Micron for the technology transfer of 64K DRAM design and manufacturing. Samsung engineers were given only very basic technology training and had to abide by strict rules set by Micron. They were told not to touch any computer system and couldn't have access to any process or design office. Yet, later Korean reporters wrote, "Their eyes were sparkling like people who were looking for treasures. Their ears worked like high-fidelity recorders." After a full day of training, Samsung engineers convened again at the hotel, discussed the technology, drew the semiconductor lines based on the mental images captured during the day, and transferred the diagram to their team in Korea that night.

The rest is industry history. Samsung became No. 1 in the memory business in 1993 and is second only to Intel in the overall semiconductor market in 2013. Interestingly, *feng-shui* and naming experts claim that Samsung's Giheung* fab site was pre-destined to be a promised land for a prosperous semiconductor business. Koreans take the name of a person or a business seriously because names have meanings that can carry the spirit with them. *Feng-shui*, a Chinese system of geomancy, is also important for a house, an office or a factory as it is believed to determine the health and wealth of its occupants.

---

### A PROSPEROUS BOWL

*__Giheung__* (器興): The literal meanings of the two Chinese characters are "bowl" and "prosper." It is unusual for a city to use the character of a bowl for its name. One interpretation of *Giheung*: memory is a modern-day bowl that holds information. So *Giheung's* prosperity for the memory business was pre-destined in its name.

---

## CHAPTER 5

# 1993—Change Everything Except Your Wife and Children

1993 was the year of Samsung's "cultural revolution." KH was a man on a mission. He embarked on a global road show from Osaka, Japan to Frankfurt, Germany for four months. In Frankfurt, he summoned 200 top executives of the Samsung Group to the Kempinski Hotel Gravenbuch and held meetings with them every day for 68 days. He spoke to 1,800 Samsung leaders and employees in Japan, the USA, the UK, and Germany. He had one goal—WAKE UP, Samsung people. He told them to "change everything except your wife and children." His words became known as the Frankfurt Declaration.

The meetings were very intense and lasted long hours. A former Samsung executive recalled that one of the Frankfurt hotel managers had asked attendees, "Which religious group do you belong to?" KH felt that nothing had changed since 1987 when he became the Chairman of Samsung and declared the 2nd Start-Up of Samsung. In 1990, he even shuffled top executives to facilitate changes, but was distressed and "felt betrayed" about the lack of change. Later he confessed that he had suffered from insomnia for several months due to the fear of Samsung disappearing from the earth.

In order to announce a "cultural revolution" at Samsung, KH chose Frankfurt for two reasons. He wanted to avoid unwanted attention in two countries with Samsung competitors—the United States and Japan. It was also considered a symbolic gesture—to remind Samsung executives of the "Miracle on the Rhine River" that rebuilt West Germany from the ashes of World War II. Later Korea's accomplishment after the Korean War (1950-1953) was called the "Miracle on the Han River" after the river that divides Seoul between the north and the south.

One of the biggest facilitators of this mega change was a 13-page report known as the "Fukuda Report." Mr. Tamio Fukuda, former designer of Japanese corporations such as Kyocera and NEC, was then one of the Japanese technical advisors at Samsung. After a full-day group strategy meeting in Osaka, KH asked Japanese advisors only to remain in the room. It started at 6:00 PM and ended at 5:00 AM the next morning. KH asked them to candidly share their observations about Samsung's problems. They were hesitant to tell the truth in the beginning, but KH insisted. Soon it became a Samsung-bashing session. Fukuda turned in a report he had prepared. He had shared his observation and feedback with other SEC leaders in the past, but nothing happened. So KH was the last resort. KH read the report on the way to Frankfurt.

Some believe that report changed the fortunes of Samsung and Sony. In the report, Fukuda suggested improving Samsung's design process and innovation-thought process. He pointed out the gap between management and the design team. He was ready to tender his resignation letter, thinking that he might be fired from being so straightforward. Instead, it has been reported that he was rewarded with a huge bonus.

To send a strong message that he meant business this time, KH used shock therapy, starting Samsung's workday at 7:00 AM and ending it at 4:00 PM. He believed that long hours of Samsung men were not productive. He saw the importance of changing physical habits of employees to bring organizational changes. Certainly getting up at dawn to get to work by 7:00 AM did it. KH was willing to bet his own career on transforming Samsung. He promised that he was going to resign from Samsung if he couldn't bring results at Samsung within 10 years. "Change starts with me," declared KH. He wanted to live what Gandhi taught: "Be the change you wish to see in the world."

It's not an accident that in 1993, Samsung launched its SH-700 phone with a goal to "kick Motorola out of the Korean mobile market." Motorola was then the number one mobile phone company, yet Samsung was determined to make a dent with the model known as "AnyCall." Samsung acquired a 10% market share in the Korean market in that year, and secured the top spot in 1995. Samsung appealed to Koreans with a slogan "The Phone Is Powerful in the Korean Terrain." The marketing tactic worked because Korea consists of 70% mountains and consumers could experience better connection in the mountainous terrain. This success gave Samsung confidence to pursue the global market.

# SHOPPING WITH A PURPOSE

According to Myung-Kwan Hyun, a former chief of the Samsung Chairman's Office, the New Management had already started in Los Angeles in January 1993. Samsung Group Presidents were summoned to Los Angeles where KH was on a business trip. Upon arrival, they were given money and told to go shopping at the department stores and marts in the area. They wondered why they had to come to LA for shopping, but they went shopping anyway. The problem was evident the next day. KH poured questions to the presidents of electronics-related companies of Samsung: "Where were Samsung TVs displayed on the shelf?" "How much was the price difference from the first class products like Sony?" and "What brand did sales clerks recommend?" They saw Samsung products sitting in the back shelves with dust on them while Japanese brands were on the front shelves. On the following day, KH had a hotel ballroom rented to display TVs, refrigerators, washers, and electric ranges of competing brands. His interrogation of Samsung executives continued: "Which button on the TV remote control do people use the most?" and "Why are Samsung products treated as third class?" He wanted Samsung leaders to see the reality of Samsung's brand in the global market, when they were proud of their No.1 position in Korea.

## CHAPTER 6

# 1996—Design or Resign

*"Win customers in 0.6 seconds. There are 30,000 stimulants in 30 seconds."*

— KH Lee

"**D**esign or Resign" was a slogan created by the late British Prime Minister Margaret Thatcher in the 1980s. SEC declared 1996 the year of design revolution to boost its competitiveness through the soft power of design. KH believed that design would be the most important factor to the success of a product. "Function or quality will become less important as similar technologies will be used for most products. So what matters will be unique design that will help customers express themselves," said he. KH noted that the concept of a consumer who just consumed a product was being replaced by the concept of a customer whose individual tastes had to be met [through customization]. If ten people liked the same color in the past, now one person wants to use ten different colors to show their unique personality.

According to Mr. Fukuda, who was the catalyst for Samsung's cultural revolution, "Design innovation (at a company) requires comprehensive innovation, so the pressure (and support) from the top is a must to make it happen." Later in 2001, KH invited Fukuda to dinner and asked him what needed to be done at Samsung. Fukuda recommended benchmarking Fabrica, founded by the Italian brand Benetton in 1994. According to its website, Fabrica is an applied creativity laboratory, a talent incubator, a studio of sorts in which young, modern artists come from all over the world to develop innovative projects and explore new directions in countless avenues of communication from design, music and film to photography, publishing and the Internet. Samsung had already been running the "Samsung Art Design Institute"

15

since 1995 and offered a three-year program in collaboration with the Parsons' New School of Design. SEC also had a design talent development program called "Design Membership" which was launched in 1993. That provided talented college students with a "creative spirit" with opportunities to explore their creativity.

KH was like Winston Churchill who famously said, "My tastes are simple. I'm easily satisfied with the best." KH had a penchant for the best things in life, from $25,000 Lansmere wool suits to $5,000 bottles of wine. KH appreciated good designs, and he wanted to add a design edge to Samsung products. Samsung soon created the Innovative Design Lab and recruited international faculty members to develop Samsung design talent. He also sent Samsung designers to the fashion mecca Milan and other places in vogue to study the latest global trends. Samsung also opened design centers in strategic locations, including San Francisco, London, Milan and Tokyo. Each site had a specific purpose to leverage its unique strengths of local talent and tradition. For example,

- USA: digital trends and the soft side of design
- UK: design strategies
- Italy: fashionable designs
- Japan: enhanced usability and an innovative finishing touch.

Other changes included creating a Chief Design Officer position and adopting a design archive system. The latter was to first create designs with which they would work out the details later for product applications. In 2005, KH hosted a design management strategy meeting in Milan and declared it the year of the 2nd Design Revolution. All of these investments paid off, and Samsung products started winning prestigious design awards across the globe.

Even with those successes, Samsung is still working on four things that KH demanded:

- Unique Samsung identity for all products
- Design talent recruitment and development
- Creative and flexible culture
- Strengthening infrastructure to support the production of a premium design brand.

## CHAPTER 7

# 1997—Transform Dangers into Opportunities

*"The stronger the wind, the higher a kite will fly."*

— KH Lee

During the 1997 Asian financial crisis, Korea was on the verge of economic collapse. With the massive layoffs and unprecedented restructuring at corporations, Koreans made fun of the IMF (International Monetary Fund) as the acronym for I'M Fired. That was the end of the Korean conglomerates' (known as *chaebol*) traditional practice of life-long employment and their employees' loyalty to the *chaebol*. After the crisis, Korean corporate warriors no longer believed that a company would take care of them until retirement. Although the Chinese word for crisis (危機) consists of the characters for danger and opportunity, even optimistic Koreans found it difficult to see opportunities in such perils.

Interestingly, it was reported that KH had sensed that something would happen before the millennium. In 1996, he ordered Samsung leaders to be in "crisis management mode." As a result Samsung was prepared to deal with the crisis and used it as a facilitator of transformation. To manage the crisis, KH asked Samsung's restructuring group to work on two things: focus and choice. He entrusted them with the execution of details, but he also brought in a foreign restructuring company to Korea and asked them to do anything they wanted with all Samsung entities except Samsung Electronics and Samsung C&T Corporation. The group consolidated businesses and shed non-profitable businesses.

Over 20% of employees were released, and executives took salary reductions. Samsung employees could no longer expect "lifelong employment" either. Like most

17

Korean corporate employees, they also learned the importance of "portable skills" for lifelong employability as more Korean employers were adopting evaluations based on performance rather than seniority. Samsung became stronger after the crisis. Hak-Soo Lee, then the group's leader known as KH's other half, was credited for keeping Samsung strong. As a finance expert, he daily monitored the cash flow of Samsung subsidiaries so that they could avoid debt with high interest rates.

When the world economy suffered from the recession in the late 2000s, financial leaders of the world predicted that Korea would weather the storm better than other countries. And it did, because "Tough times never last, but tough people do." And Samsung certainly toughened their "stress resistance muscles" by managing an earlier crisis and on-going, self-imposed "perpetual crises." In the wake of the recent crisis, SEC's profits were higher than the combined profits of the five largest Japanese electronics firms (Sony, Panasonic, Toshiba, Hitachi and Sharp), according to a *Harvard Business Review* article on Samsung. The "Three Stars" of Samsung shone brighter during dark periods because Samsung people had been trained to embrace change and prepare themselves for any adversity.

## CHAPTER 8

# 2003—Discover Three Geniuses and China

*"In ten years, even the mountains and rivers will change."*

— Korean proverb

Celebrating its 30th Anniversary in 1999, SEC shared its vision to become a company that will lead the Digital Convergence Revolution. Samsung moved mountains and changed the river flows for the first ten years since KH declared the New Management 1.0 in 1993. By 2003, Sony and Panasonic were no longer big players for Samsung. Given the changes in the global electronics industry landscape, Samsung announced the New Management 2.0 in 2003 with three specific goals:

- Genius management
- Discovery of future growth engines
- Strengthening China strategy.

"Genius management" was based on KH's belief that one genius would be able to provide livelihoods to 100,000 people. Citing the contributions of extraordinary technology or business geniuses, such as Bill Gates, KH emphasized the need for transformation of the Korean educational system so that such geniuses could be discovered and developed. He warned the danger of downward leveling in the Korean system that would lead to meeting the lowest common denominator under the name of "equal opportunities." Given SEC's 240,000 global employees, SEC would need at least three geniuses that will take care of its future.

KH also stressed the importance of discovering new growth engines that would bring big revenue to Samsung. By 2004, SEC surpassed $10 billion in net profit on $55.2 billion in revenue, second only to Toyota in terms of manufacturing profitability. In 2006, it ranked third in the global TV markets, but KH was looking for "future business" items. Samsung has identified five key "Life Care" businesses as areas for investment: biochip, medical equipment, U-health, solar and I-Robot. Samsung is continuously watching market trends and readjusting its course to achieve Samsung's long-term vision.

In 2003 China no longer was a place for cheap labor, but became a strategic market for SEC. KH ordered his staff to strengthen Samsung's China strategy and said, "Current elementary school students won't be able to get a job if they can't speak Chinese by the time they look for employment." Not surprisingly, JY, the only son of KH and Vice Chairman of SEC, has been building key relationships in China. The report that JY's son is attending a middle school in China indicates Samsung's long-term vision for China. Samsung leaders are studying China-related subjects, including ancient leadership principles and current Chinese leaders' styles and policies.

The duty free shops of Shilla Hotel, a Samsung company managed by KH's first daughter, are already a beneficiary of China's rising middle class and their appetite for luxury. Shilla owns a duty free shop in Suzhou, China where it has a luxury hotel and SEC has significant operations. Korea's Incheon International Airport has the highest duty-free sales in the world and Chinese spending in Korean duty free shops has surpassed Japanese consumption. Thanks to KH's earlier vision for a China strategy, Samsung will likely reach $100 billion sales in China in the near future.

## CHAPTER 9

# 2013—Be More Paranoid at the Top

*"Samsung was bankrupt in 1986.... Now is not the time that we will try our best or not. Our choice: change or die."*

— KH Lee

In June 2013, Samsung hosted an international academic conference on innovation in celebration of the 20th anniversary of Samsung's New Management, which started in 1993. KH didn't attend it and left for Japan that day. Some interpreted his absence as his resolve to plan for the next 20 years, rather than resting on the laurels of accomplishment from the first two decades after the "cultural revolution."

Dominating the smartphone and TV markets with record profits, Samsung was at the top of the world. Samsung Electronics recorded the world's third largest market capitalization in the global information technology (IT) sector as of late 2012. And it became the world's first electronics company to exceed $200 billion of sales revenue in 2013. The target date for that goal was originally 2015, when then SEC Vice Chairman Gee-Sung Choi announced it in 2011. Yet Samsung is more paranoid than ever.

Samsung certainly knows how to be an overachiever with paranoia. "Even first-class companies are collapsing. Nobody knows about Samsung's future either. Most businesses and products that represent Samsung will disappear within ten years. So we must start over," declared KH when he returned to the CEO role in March 2010 after a two-year leave of absence. More recently KH warned Samsung executives and employees of a danger of arrogance and self-satisfaction. They are in crisis mode because "those who climb the mountain must be prepared to come down." Korea's *Maeil Economic Daily* reported that SEC broadcasts messages to employees that remind them of the fall of Sony and Nokia.

Even if Samsung posted record profits in 2013, Samsung leaders were concerned about being overly dependent on its telecommunications portfolio. Despite SEC's sales revenue and operating profit increasing by 14% and 27% respectively from 2012, an SEC group-wise strategy team representing all business units has been exploring new areas for convergence and synergy. They have also been researching future business items including multi-device options, mobile health, 3D printing, future TVs and an integrated contents platform. These are different from the five "new growth engines" identified in the past. Samsung is also venturing into the drug industry. Some see that Samsung BioLogics may become a TSMC (Taiwan Semiconductor Manufacturing Company, the world's first dedicated semiconductor foundry) of the pharmaceutical industry to build a strong business by applying its technical expertise in high-quality manufacturing for global pharmaceutical companies.

Reaching the middle age of 40 in 2009, SEC declared 2010 as a year of transformation from the old Samsung to a new Samsung: from fast follower to first mover, in all categories such as mobile phones, consumer electronics and semiconductors. They were once dreams, but are now becoming realities. Samsung has even more ambitious plans to become a respectable first mover. To plant seeds for new venture DNA, SEC announced a $1 billion investment in venture funding in February 2013. Under the new initiative, Samsung will seek M&A (merger & acquisition) deals with global venture companies Its target areas include cloud computing, the Internet of Things, mobile security, mobile health and technology with emotional factors. Samsung's acquisitions of U.S. companies such as Shelvy TV, SmartThings, and Quietside in 2014 demonstrate its commitment to find new growth engines through M&A.

Samsung also wants to create a new business ecosystem around its semiconductors and electronic parts in order to provide customers with new value, new experiences and a new culture. SEC strives to be born again as a "Market Creator" by preparing for bad times in good times and anticipating good times in bad times. For transformation, Samsung demonstrates KH's mantra: "Change in the times of highest performance."

## CHAPTER 10

# 2020—Inspire the World, Create the Future

"Inspire the World, Create the Future" is Samsung's vision for the decade. Samsung is one of the few companies that shares its long-term vision with the public with online posts. It set a 2010 Vision, a 2015 Vision and a 2020 Vision several years in advance. Neither Apple nor Intel mentions its vision for a specific year on its website, although the late Steve Jobs was known for his long-term vision for products.

In 1995 when its revenue was only one-tenth of Sony's, Samsung's desire to "Beat Sony" was a known "secret." That dream became a reality in 2002. By 2005, its revenue was double that of Sony. Samsung's vision was not just to increase revenue or beat its competition. Samsung was obsessed with improving quality and brand. In 2006, it had a vision to be the "Mercedes of IT."

Samsung leaders seem to believe that a 30% sales increase is easier to accomplish than a 5% increase because people try harder with a seemingly impossible goal. Thus, Samsung has been setting "ridiculously" aggressive goals and has delivered them year after year. Now that "Beat Apple" has been met, some speculate that Samsung's new motto must be "Beat Intel."

Vision 2020 was declared in 2009 on SEC's 40th anniversary and the specific goals have been imprinted in the heads of Samsung leaders. Leveraging its three key strengths—"new technology," "innovative products" and "creative solutions," Samsung envisions the following by 2020:

- $400 billion revenue
- Top 10 Global Corporation

- Top 5 brands in the world (# 8 in 2013 up from # 9 in 2012 by Interbrand)
- Formidable No. 1 IT Leader
- The World's Most Admired Companies Top 10 (#35 in 2013 by Fortune, moving up from #37 in 2012).

In order to reinforce their vision, Samsung hosted a two-day "Mach Forum" in early 2014 for its Executive Vice Presidents, Senior Vice Presidents, and Vice Presidents.

---

## MACH MANAGEMENT

"Mach Management" is a concept KH introduced in 2006, and was emphasized again in 2014 in his New Year Message to Samsung global employees. This initiative is based on the idea that a jet has to not only upgrade its engine but also change blueprints, materials and systems in order to fly faster at supersonic speeds. Likewise, if Samsung is to become a world-class company, Samsung needs to bring in comprehensive and fundamental changes, including its structure and management practices.

---

To ensure efficient execution of "Mach Management," Samsung reshuffled its Future Strategy Office known as Samsung's "Control Tower" effective May 2014 and changed six out of its seven team leaders. Its top executives for personnel affairs and communication have been sent to SEC in order to strengthen "field management" and infrastructure for Samsung's management support. This announcement was totally unexpected because the annual executive appointments were made only five months ago. KH again showed his commitment to change and demonstrated decisive and speedy decision-making that will enable Samsung's 2020 vision.

# II

# Founder's Legacy— The Midas Hands of Byung-Chull Lee

## CHAPTER 11

# Read the Times for the Right Timing

As a "genius entrepreneur," BC focused on "reading the times," scanning the environment and forecasting the trends. After the Korean War, BC saw what Koreans needed. That's why his business dealt with the commodities (rice, sugar, fertilizer and textiles). The founder's legacy of accurately reading the times has helped SEC stay ahead of the curve and become a market leader in LED TVs, 3D TVs, Smart TVs and OLED TVs. Before the days of the Internet, BC used newspapers as an important source of gathering information. An employee was dedicated to compiling the list of important articles from all the major newspapers of Korea and Japan. He underlined newsworthy items in red and provided BC with a summary.

To read the times, BC spent major holidays at the beginning and the end of each year in Tokyo, Japan. The latter part was known as "BC's Tokyo Strategic Thinking Session." During his stay, he faithfully watched the New Year's Special TV programs featuring renowned scholars and journalists in Japan. They discussed global business trends and forecasted the Japanese economy for the upcoming year.

After BC gained an understanding of the big picture, he scheduled one-on-one meetings with Japanese journalists who covered the economy. BC, who spoke Japanese, asked them: "What kind of business was good last year? What is the growth forecast for the New Year? What would be the reasons for growth?" Then, he invited scholars who understood not only the theory of economics, but also the reality of management. Lastly, he met with outstanding business leaders who could provide success factors with concrete examples. These meetings were possible because of his strong network in Japanese academia, media and industry in addition to his Japanese language competency.

When he returned to Korea in mid-January, he had his staff conduct feasibility studies of the business items he identified for benchmarking. "A real businessman doesn't attach any meaning to a good economy (boom) or a bad economy (recession)," said Konosuke Matsushita, founder of Panasonic. BC found opportunities in all seasons.

According to BC, success is not determined by one's competencies alone, but by luck and good timing. BC summarized success factors in business with three Chinese characters:

運鈍根

- *The first character is luck.*

- *The literal meaning of the second is "not sharp", and can be translated as patient. If one wants to succeed, he needs to wait until the right timing when luck comes to him.*

- *The third one is "root" and can be interpreted as "perseverance" with strong conviction.*

  *Without patience and perserverance one will miss the opportunities to get lucky.*

Bill Gates also frequently credited his success to luck. Interestingly, Hyundai founder Joo-Young Jeong said, "Unless you think that you are unlucky, there is no such thing as bad luck." Successful people must know how to create their own luck with patience, hard work and perseverance.

## CHAPTER 12

# Be Preoccupied with Two Questions

BC once said, "My life is summarized with two questions:

- Which business am I going to start?
- To whom am I going to delegate it?"

If a real estate value is determined by location, BC believed that a company's talent would measure its valuation. For BC, talented professionals were not just idea makers. They also had to be aggressive executors. BC preferred those who:

- Don't seek attention to themselves, but are fully committed to execution in order to deliver results
- Give credit to others, instead of taking credit for success
- Develop successors so that the company will last even after their departure.

With a conviction that talent = company, he knew the importance of hiring the right people. Even if he was perceived as cold-blooded (especially for Korean businessmen who value humanity and warmth), he said he still didn't like firing people. Therefore, he emphasized face-to-face interviews, participated in applicant interviews and preferred clean-cut people. He thought that they tended to be honest. He watched their mouth and hand movements for their trustworthiness. It has been rumored that he even brought face readers for executive interviews. BC also examined a candidate's appearance. Once he commented on an applicant who wore shoes with soil, "That type of person doesn't belong here." BC perceived him as someone who didn't take the job seriously because he was careless about his shoes.

Many Asians tend to judge a person's character or personality based on the shapes of eyes, ears, nose and mouth as well as eyebrow thickness and even teeth alignment. A former Samsung HR executive who had interviewed job candidates concluded that people with thin lips had a tendency to be temperamental. It is fascinating that even in the U.S. and UK, researchers have found that corporate performance and CEO faces are closely related. According to Elaine M. Wong and her colleagues at the University of Wisconsin, CEOs with wider faces relative to face height delivered much better results than those with narrower faces. Asians are also big on *ki* or *chi* that emanates from a person. It is similar to the chemistry between one person and another.

It is not just Asians who value facial impressions or body languages. Abraham Lincoln once said, "A man at the age of 40 should be responsible for his face."

> *"I don't like the looks of that man," Abraham Lincoln is reported to have said to an aide.*
>
> *"A person can't help what he looks like, Mr. President," the aide replied.*
>
> *"Oh, yes, he can," Mr. Lincoln answered.*

BC and Lincoln would have gotten along well if they had ever met.

## CHAPTER 13

# Benchmark Japan

BC grew up in an affluent family and went to Japan to attend Waseda University, a prestigious private university, during the Japanese occupation of Korea (1910-1945). Unfortunately, he got ill in his first year and had to return to Korea. Yet, BC's Japanese language and cultural competency helped him watch Japanese conglomerates and benchmark them. In Korea, BC was not alone in monitoring Japan for new ideas, even if it was taboo to publicly admire anything Japanese. Older Koreans had painful memories of Japan's brutal colonization of their country, when Koreans were forced to speak Japanese and pressured to worship at Japanese Shinto shrines. As recently as the 1990s, Korean radio stations couldn't play Japanese music.

However, Koreans still followed Japanese trends, from entertainment to education. Television programs frequently imitated Japanese programs with very similar formats, plots, and stage equipment. High school seniors often reviewed the previous year's entrance examination questions (especially in mathematics) of major Japanese universities because similar questions would appear in the Korean college examinations one year later. Tutors during my high school years had us take a practice test with the questions appeared in the entrance examinations of Tokyo University in the prior year.

BC said, "To catch up with Japan, we need to know Japan" and strove to learn about and from Japan. A Japanese economist who had known BC said, "I haven't seen BC buying anything else except books and electronics in Japan." BC sought out every opportunity to learn the best practices from Japan. To offer perfect sushi at Samsung-owned Shilla Hotel in Seoul, BC even asked the chief chef of Tokyo's top Okura Hotel about the number of rice grains and the temperature of boiling water. The Lee family's "Japan learning" efforts have continued for three generations: BC sent his three sons to Japan for study and KH sent his son JY to Japan for an MBA at Keio University.

In his biography, BC recollected his trip to Japan in February 1950: Japanese industry leaders invited him and 15 other Korean businessmen to explore business opportunities with Korea. After World War II, Japan wasn't inspiring; the ruins of buildings, factories and houses were everywhere. One evening toward the end of his trip, he went into a barbershop in Akasaka, Tokyo. On the door, there was a nameplate of "Morita." BC asked the owner who was cutting his hair, "How long have you been in this business?" "I am the third generation, so it must be at least 60 years and I hope that my son will inherit the business," replied the barber in his 40s. Given Morita's answer, BC saw the possibility that Japan's sun would rise again. He was inspired by the Japanese spirit of a true craftsman, which was passed on from one generation to the next. Japan's *"shokunin"* represented a mastery of one's profession, commitment to delivering a product or service of the highest quality with the dedication to enhance the lives of people. BC wanted such a professional spirit at Samsung.

Thus, it is not surprising that Samsung was similar to Japanese corporations during the reign of BC. It was believed that even Samsung's training programs in the 1970s and 1980s had been modeled after Japanese corporate training programs. This was different from Hyundai, which had a more home-grown corporate culture of Korea. According to the article "The Paradox of Samsung's Rise" in *Harvard Business Review*, Samsung rose to prominence in Korea under the Japanese model of unrelated diversification and vertical integration in pursuit of synergies. Samsung built its corporate muscle in industries that Japan once dominated: consumer electronics, memory chips and LCD panels. Diversification served Samsung and other Korean companies well, because it allowed them to use internally-generated cash from one operation to fund other operations. The Japanese hierarchical labor model also worked in the Korean context because employee mobility was rare.

Ironically, BC's benchmarking Japan set a foundation for "Benchmarking Korea" by Japanese electronics manufacturers half a century later. "Japanese firms were too confident about our technology and manufacturing prowess. We lost sight of the products from the consumer's point of view," said Panasonic CEO Kazuhiro Tsuga in 2012. A *Wall Street Journal* article concurred: "Japan's current weakness is rooted in its traditional strength: a fixation with the art of making things, focused on hardware advances, neglecting the factors that really mattered to people such as design and ease of use." It is common that overused strengths of individuals or corporations often become their liabilities.

## CHAPTER 14

# Tap All Bridges Before Crossing

When Koreans compared Samsung's and Hyundai's corporate cultures during BC's era, some used an analogy of running a marathon. Samsung runners would analyze all of the terrain, weather and other elements, but Hyundai runners would start running first and analyze those while running. BC learned the importance of planning and prudence from his failures in early ventures of rice trading and real estate. Based on the lessons he gained from failures, he set a few principles for running a business, including:

- Scan the business environment clearly.
- Control greed and know your capabilities and limitations.
- Avoid any investment that relies on wishful thinking and pure luck.
- Develop intuition, but create the 2nd and 3rd contingency plans. If the situation doesn't look favorable or ends in failure, forget the past with decisive courage and move on with the best option.

When BC founded the Cheil Industries, a Samsung company dealing with textiles and chemicals, he listed 48 items to examine and identified potential problems and solutions. The items included temperature, humidity, electricity, water quality, transportation, work force, employee training, etc. In contrast, Joo-Young Jeong, founder of Hyundai Group, was an optimist and believed that success would follow if he stayed positive and made the effort. He said, "I have started every project with 90% conviction that it can be done and 10% self-confidence that I will make it happen. There is no room for even one percent of doubt." As a master of "Can Do" spirit, Jeong's famous quote was, "Have you tried it?"

Given that kind of perfectionism, BC couldn't stand any inaccuracy in forecasting. In his book, Chang-Woo Lee, a former advisor to BC, recalled a meeting between BC and an executive who was reporting to BC about the success of a new business.

*BC: You had a $20 million loss?*

*Executive: No, we had a $30 million profit.*

*BC: Didn't you say that the original profit forecast was $50 million?*

*Executive: Yes.*

*BC: Then, isn't it a loss since you earned only $30 million?*

*Executive: No. We expected to earn $50 million, but the operating profit was $30 million.*

*BC: If that's the case, did you inflate the forecast?*

*Executive: No. It was correct at the time of forecasting.*

*BC: I don't understand. Your forecasting was accurate. If nothing went wrong, how can you earn less than forecasting? Why don't you go back and think about what went wrong?*

*Executive: Originally we were planning to launch the products in the beginning of February. But due to a delay in parts delivery and the production schedule, the project was delayed for five months. That means there was lack of collaboration among product planning, manufacturing, research, and purchasing. So next time I'll improve their collaboration and meet the launch date.*

*BC: I get it. It's commendable that you made a $30 million profit for the first production. Yet if your original goal was $50 million, you have to study the reasons why the goal wasn't met. Instead, you skipped the topic and focused on the profit. Often people think that it doesn't matter because ends results are not bad. But this becomes a bigger problem. So it is important to reflect on the result.*

## CHAPTER 15

# It Is I Who Give Orders

O ne of Samsung's success factors is strong and speedy decision-making by its owners. Even if SEC is a public company, the founder's family members still rule the company, as KH, JY and other Samsung entities hold a 17.65% stake (as of early 2014). BC was quoted saying, "It is I who give orders." Fortunately, he sought out input and listened to others first before he made any decision. He also relied on dedicated leaders who disseminated his orders and faithful followers executed them. As a perfectionist, BC built an organizational structure of centralized control and management.

Created in 1959, the Chairman's Office of Staff exercised enormous and absolute power in the Samsung Group. They guarded and protected BC. They were extremely loyal. Their stature in Samsung was unchallenged. During its heyday, the Office had over 200 brains in charge of strategic planning, corporate intelligence, finance, human resources, public relations, international trade, technology development and auditing. With its power, prestige and ability to influence Samsung's big picture, it was considered the most coveted office. They controlled the group's money and talent, and their power also derived from auditing. So BC had to be sensitive to the dynamics between them and other Samsung executives.

Once, BC heard about the "sky high" power of his Chief of Staff. The Presidents of Samsung subsidiaries, who were higher in rank and grade than the Chief, felt that he was over-domineering and controlling. BC summoned him and asked him in his provincial dialect, "What is your title?" "I'm a Vice President," he answered. "OK, a VP." BC repeated, "It is correct that you are a VP." It was an indirect warning to the Chief of Staff to know his place and not to overpower Samsung Presidents (using his office). Still, even division Presidents went to "mock meetings" held by the Chief of Staff to prepare answers to BC's questions. They were so secretive and powerful that some called it the Gestapo, the official secret police of Nazi Germany and German-occupied Europe.

KH didn't like the office and weakened its power when he became Chairman. He saw it as a barrier to effective organizational communication because they controlled and filtered the messages to the top. Thus, he replaced most of the top 20 leaders at the office two years after he became Chairman. It was the largest organizational change in the history of that office and sent a strong signal of his determination to transform the old Samsung from BC days.

After the Asian financial crisis in 1997, the office was renamed to the Headquarters of Organizational Restructuring. It was then changed to the Office of Future Strategy. Despite the changes in its size and name, it has been considered the most powerful group in Samsung. The former head of the office was known as the right hand of KH, so enterprise or division Presidents often followed the directions from the office. Although the management styles of BC and KH were different, both father and son knew how to demand absolute loyalty and followership from their lieutenants.

# Delegate Only If You Trust

Leaders who have a tendency for control often find it difficult to delegate, especially if they had a successful track record. BC believed in delegating 100% to people whom he could trust. He learned this valuable lesson from his heartfelt experience. During the Korean War (1950-1953), BC lost everything in Seoul and went to Daegu, a southeast part of Korea close to his birthplace, where he had entrusted a business with a manager before his move to Seoul years earlier. He jumped for joy with tears when he found that the manager had earned and saved enough money for him to rebuild Samsung. Since then, his motto for talent management was:

> *"If you hired someone with trust, utilize him. If you can't trust a person, don't hire him."*

There was no line for BC's signature on Samsung's approval form. He left it to professional managers and subject-matter experts and strictly used a merit-based system for executive promotions. Despite the fact that Korean culture was more relationship-oriented than task-oriented, such factors as blood relations, regional ties or school ties didn't matter much at Samsung. BC made sure that executives were accountable for results. If he wasn't sure if a person could do a good job, he placed "two in a box" (before Intel adopted the practice). "Everyone has a weakness or two. It is hard for one to change his behaviors in order to correct them. So I appoint two people for one position so that they can complement each other's weaknesses," said BC. He was an organizational development (OD) specialist without formal training.

Even when leadership and communication style assessment tools such as DISC or Insights were not available in Korea, he accurately assessed the styles of his lieutenants and used them for the roles that best utilized their personalities. He optimized the effectiveness of his team with diverse leaders who were visionary, analytical or results-oriented. BC had a clear principle for rewarding winners and punishing losers. Some perceived his practice as "the winner takes all;" however, he was willing to keep the executives who tried earnestly and failed. Even in asking for accountability, he sprinkled wisdom for discipline:

> *"When you are questioning a leader for accountability, don't overdo it. Leave some room for him to escape (or save face). Don't push someone to the brink of self-despair and giving up. It's desirable to give him an opportunity to recover from it and motivate himself again."*

## CHAPTER 17

# Spend 80% of Your Time
# Developing Talent

"**P**eople say money begets money. But I believe it's neither money nor power that makes money. It's people," said BC. He was religious about developing talent and spent 80% of his time developing talent. He believed that business would endlessly prosper when a leader commits himself to talent development with all of his heart. What kind of talent did he want?

- Idea-makers
- Aggressive and execution-oriented employees
- Team players with a strong sense of accountability

Samsung's learning and development programs were cutting edge for Korean companies, thanks to BC's commitment to developing people. As a life-long learner, he knew the importance of investing in employee education. He hung new-hire training schedules on his wall and checked with HR leaders to see how each training program went. When executive coaching was uncommon even in the West, he hired industrial psychologists and listened to their advice on talent development.

He was not a micromanager, but he had a hands-on approach for critical matters: He reviewed course materials for executive curriculum and asked experts to create a training course for newly appointed Presidents. The key theme was how a leader could connect the people in an organization (employees) with the people in a market (customers). To focus on people rather than numbers was a unique approach. Topics included: time management, setting priorities and dos and don'ts for Presidents. Considering that the concept of time management was popularized in Korea only in the early 1990s, BC and Samsung were well ahead of the times. If GE's success was due to its learning culture, Samsung also shared that culture.

An avid reader, BC frequently brought books from Japan for his executives and ordered them to write reports about the books. Samsung Presidents' weekly meetings have also been used for executive development and internal collaboration. Every Wednesday, the Presidents of Samsung subsidiaries gathered together for a seminar and discussion. Even now, Samsung CEOs and Presidents meet on every Wednesday morning at Samsung Headquarters.

BC's "talent first" policy was extended to create an environment where good people were motivated. His goal was to take care of employees' benefits and compensation before they would ask for them.

---

## FIRST-CLASS FACTORY DORMITORIES

BC demanded a first-class dormitory for female factory workers, equipped with western style heating, baths and restrooms. He had trees planted and added a pond and a fountain to make the factory atmosphere pleasant. When some executives complained why he would waste money for unnecessary "luxuries," BC assured them, "In the long run, this is a service to society. When the productivity of female factory workers increases, production cost will decrease and the price of a product will go down."

---

## CHAPTER 18

# Listen with Respect

It has been reported that on a wall at KH's home office there is a calligraphy scroll with these two Chinese characters (敬聽). The first one means respect and the second means listening. BC wrote the characters himself and gave the scroll to KH on his first day of work at Samsung. BC was a devoted student of the ancient Chinese philosopher Confucius, who said, "If I walk with two other men, each of them will serve as my teacher." Thus, BC saw the benefits of listening, and he emphasized that skill to his son and successor. Considering that numerous global leaders receive coaching to improve their listening skills, BC's advice to his son was invaluable.

Senior Korean leaders were often authoritarian. However, two charismatic leaders, BC and Joo-Young Jeong, the founder of Hyundai Group, knew how to listen. BC sought out and listened to those who had different ideas from his. Jeong frequently quoted Confucius: "It's not a shame to ask someone who is younger and lower in status." And when he asked, he listened attentively.

BC also believed that one would find something useful from listening to another, regardless of age, title, and status. He used every opportunity to learn from others. He especially appreciated stories based on real life or field experience. If a foreign CEO requested a visit, he studied the CEO's companies and their revenues, market shares, profits and losses before the visit. Then he was able to ask the right questions and listen for insight. After such a meeting, a CEO of a U.S. multinational said, "I feel as if I had a job interview. But I respect BC's sincere desire to know about my company. If we were to start a business in Korea, we will consider Samsung first as our partner." To lead companies well, CEOs must be Chief Listening Officers (CLOs).

# HOW TO LISTEN

The ancient Chinese character for listening contains radicals that respectively mean king, ear, ten, eye, one and heart. That can be interpreted as "pay undivided attention with ears like a king's ten eyes and one heart."

# HOW TO IMPROVE YOUR LISTENING SKILLS

- Monitor your talking/listening ratio. Set the goal at 5 to 5 or 3 to 7 (if you are known for talking too much).
- Think before you speak.
- Be genuinely interested in a different perspective.
- Focus on what is said, instead of your next words.
- Show a sincere desire to see from other perspectives.
- Avoid, "Yes, but." Instead try, "What I like about that idea is…"
- Do not interrupt.
- Find ways to contribute meaningfully. Don't feel compelled to have opinions about everything.
- Don't try to defend your position.

## CHAPTER 19

# Only the Best-in-Class Will Survive

Accoording to people who knew BC, he was like a clock. He got up at 6:00 AM and listed all of the things he needed to do for the day. He came home at 6:00 PM, bathed at 8:00 PM and went to bed at 10:00 PM. Even his bath water had to be prepared at the same temperature every evening. He could tell if there was even a one-degree difference. If he didn't like the way his memo was written, he tore it up and wrote another. The leader's habit of thorough planning and attention to detail became a part of Samsung's DNA. BC ordered Samsung products and services to be made with the same perfection and meticulous detail.

When a gallery for his collections was built in the 1970s, he requested that it be constructed to endure for 1,000 years without any repair. He liked to collect artwork and antiques, many of which were Korean national treasures. He dressed like a man in GQ magazine, compared with his contemporary business hero from Hyundai, Joo-Young Jeong who called himself "a rich blue-collar worker" and wore 20-year-old shoes with holes. BC used handmade premium clubs for his golf and once he had more than 500 of the best name brand clubs. He wore only premium golf shoes and used the best balls. For his meals, he appreciated quality more than quantity.

Some people criticized his "aristocratic" taste, but BC's preference for high quality products and services reflected his desire to know their differentiators: what made one better than others. He analyzed where and how these world-class products had been made. This reminds me of my interview with Dr. Soon Cho, former Korean deputy prime minister in the early 1990s. During that time, Korean media condemned Koreans' purchases of expensive foreign products as if those behaviors were unpatriotic. Dr. Cho, a renowned economist, shared a different perspective: "If we Koreans want to make better quality products to compete in the global market, we have to have first-hand experience in using well-made products." His view was similar to advice which Mr. Akio Morita, former CEO of Sony, received from his Japanese-American advisor when he came to the U.S. for business: "Stay at the best hotel and eat at the best restaurant to experience the best and to know what makes them stand out." BC must have had more high-end product experience than most Koreans.

Even in the beginning of his career, BC had an ambitious vision to make Samsung No. 1. In addition to the name Samsung, he used Cheil (literally meaning number one in Korean with Chinese characters) for several enterprises, such as a sugar company (which later became a part of CJ Group, a conglomerate run by BC's first grandson), a textile company, and an advertising agency. It showed his desire to be the best in any business he entered. Samsung has been striving to reach the top in every category in which they compete. According to Korean reporters who covered Samsung, Cheil was not a slogan at Samsung. It was a religion.

## CHAPTER 20

# Merit First, Even for Family Succession Planning

One of the key Korean values is relationship-orientation based on blood relation, hometown connection and school ties. With a saying that arms bend inward, many Koreans tend to give and receive favors to and from the people who share common backgrounds. For example, the government of former President Myung-Bak Lee was criticized for appointing people who were from his hometown province, his college alma mater and his church to key government positions. That is one of the reasons why Korean parents are eager to send their children to top schools. They want their children to make lifetime connections that can be used for their business and career development. As in many relationship-oriented cultures, network is net worth in Korea.

Samsung was a little different. BC emphasized strictly merit-based hiring and promotion—even when it came to his family. BC's succession planning was not an exception. He had three sons and five daughters from his Korean wife. Traditionally in Korea, it was a norm that a family business went to the first son. However, BC had a conflict with his first son. "I let him run a business unit for six months, but he failed," said BC. The second son who studied in Japan and married a Japanese woman was also strong-willed and considered unfit for leading Samsung.

Shortly before his operation for cancer in 1976, he summoned his wife and children and announced that Samsung would be run by KH if anything happens to him. It was a total shock to everyone and especially his first son was speechless. BC also divided different businesses for each of his children to prevent future conflict among his descendants. He was keenly aware that Samsung could be ruined if his children were to fight against each other over their inheritance. Despite BC's planning, the first son's lawsuit against KH over inheritance in 2012 became a national soap opera in Korea.

The appointment was not an easy win for KH, even if he served as Vice Chairman under his father. For a meticulous, business-first father, he had to prove himself through rigorous checkpoints and testing. At one point, he was sent abroad with his official roles stripped away. A few executives closest to him were also removed from their key positions at Samsung. Later KH recalled the experience as one of the most difficult times of his life. BC knew that gold was tested in fire. BC must have wanted to see how KH handled himself in times of adversity: He had to be able to maintain steadiness and serenity even in such hardship. In a similar way, Hyundai's Joo-Young Jeong also emphasized keeping a cool mind in tough times:

> *"When we think too much and make things complicated, we get weak. Good ideas come from a clear mind. We become strong and steadfast when we keep our mind cool. So I encourage people to keep their mind cool."*

## A COOL MIND

The two Chinese characters (淡淡) for "keeping a cool mind" are identical. Each has three components with a character for water and two for fire: It implies a cool mind is like putting out a double fire with water.

# III

# Kun-Hee Lee:
# The CEO Nobody Knows

## CHAPTER 21

# Greater than Jack Welch?

"What's the difference between God and Larry Ellison (the Founder and Chairman of Oracle Corporation)?" an Oracle employee asked me. Before I gave my answer, she told me the joke: "God is God, and Ellison thinks that he is God." Nobody says that KH considers himself to be God; however, some people believe that KH was worshipped that way at Samsung. According to Ha-Sang Hong, an author of several books on Korean business leaders, KH and Admiral Soon-Shin Lee were the only two Koreans who won over Japan for the last 600 years. Admiral Lee was a Korean naval commander who became famous for his victories against the Japanese navy in the 16th century. That says a lot about KH's accomplishment.

It was in 1987 that KH succeeded his father as only the second Chairman in the company's history. Under his leadership, Samsung expanded its annual sales to over $353 billion. During his reign, Samsung market valuation increased by 303 times compared to 38 times the growth rate at GE under Jack Welch (for 20 years). KH's accomplishment is like a miracle, considering the problems he inherited when he took over Samsung. The authors of the *Harvard Business Review* article "Paradox of Samsung's Rise" listed the challenges that KH faced:

"Its overseas position as a low-cost producer was becoming untenable in the face of intensifying competition from Japanese electronics makers, which were setting up manufacturing plants in Southeast Asia, and rising domestic wages in South Korea's newly liberalizing economy." It was not easy to inherit a successful family business. It was even harder to create a bigger legacy than the visionary leader who happened to be his father.

Two great teachers had prepared him well for those challenges: BC, his father, and Jin-Ki Hong, his father-in-law, who was a Supreme Court judge and BC's business partner. BC asked KH to take on projects himself to get first-hand experience in running a business. He didn't give his son any specific directions or teach him what to do in certain situations. One the other hand, Hong caringly and clearly explained to KH the business environment variables and their relationships, such as politics, economics, law and government. While KH learned intuition and the micro-perspective from his father, he gained logic and the macro perspective from his father-in-law.

In his early years, KH shared some similarities with Steve Jobs. In the basement of his home, KH tore apart electronic items and reassembled them. Because of his expertise in electronics, people joke that he must have majored in electrical engineering in the College of Business at Waseda University where he was enrolled. Some say that smart and lonely people tend to fall in love with technology. He was a technology maniac and changed his cars six times during the short time he was in the U.S. for his graduate education.

Genius or near-genius, he was focused and almost obsessed with his subjects of interest. His areas of interest were long and wide, including playing table tennis, watching documentaries and breeding dogs. Once he bred 200 Jindo dogs, a breed of hunting dogs that originated from the Jindo Island of Korea, and he became an expert on that breed. A dog was his best friend and first love when he was spending his lonely childhood in Japan. Because of his experience with his aides' disloyalty, it was reported, he appreciated a dog's honesty and loyalty more than a man's capricious nature.

KH encouraged people to take "One Hobby, One Art (一趣一藝)" to improve their quality of life. He believed that playing an instrument or appreciating art would enhance one's personhood. Furthermore, he recommended them to take their hobbies seriously, do research hard, and become experts on the areas of their interest. His intense, diverse hobbies have helped him become a great leader.

## CHAPTER 22

# The Most Important Subject of My Study Is People

One of KH's high school friends recalled him saying, "The subject I'm studying the hardest is people." It is noteworthy that KH, then a young high school student, said such a thing in an incredibly competitive Korean education system where students studied academic subjects day and night. He has a unique education background for a Korean CEO. He attended part of his elementary school and middle school years in Japan. After he graduated from high school in Korea, he went to college in Japan. He then did graduate work at George Washington University in the U.S.

At a Japanese elementary school, KH must have experienced discrimination as a Korean, a citizen from a former Japanese colony. Koreans have been the biggest minority in Japan and discrimination against Koreans has been frequently reported. Masayoshi Son, CEO of SoftBank and one of the richest men in Japan, has also talked about his challenges in growing up in Japan as a Korean-Japanese. During his teenage years, Son even distanced himself from his Korean grandmother whom he had loved very much. She reminded him of *kimchi*, a fermented side dish that symbolized being a Korean, an identity which a sensitive minority teenager couldn't take pride in. After reading an inspiring book about a Japanese hero Sakamoto Ryoma who helped the transformation of Japan in the 19th Century, he was determined to dream big, instead of focusing on his "petty" personal issues like ethnicity. Son decided to go to the USA to study at the University of California at Berkeley. There he set his 50-year life plan at the age of 19: "Become famous in my 20s, accumulate hundreds of million of yen in my 30s, bet on a game-changing enterprise in my 40s, perfect the business model in my 50s, and leave it to successors in my 60s."

Son, who was born in 1959, has fulfilled these plans so far. BC and Son didn't allow their experiences to negatively shape their worldview or destiny. They accepted their realities and sought opportunities for greatness.

When KH returned to Korea for high school, his classmates teased him for speaking Korean with a Japanese accent. He didn't quite fit in either Japan or Korea. He said that the topics of his interest were different from others (Koreans) because of his overseas living experience. Having been an outsider at home and abroad, he was open to embracing people with different backgrounds. Thanks to the early exposure to foreign cultures, he also had an appreciation for diversity and inclusion and recruited "outsiders" (not typical "Samsung men" who built careers at Samsung) to join Samsung. He believed in the power of a heterogeneous team.

Despite his interest in studying people, he had such nicknames as "the hermit," "a shy prince," and the "Howard Hughes of Korea" because of his avoidance of public appearances. Some people say that he liked to play golf alone and ski alone. Prior to 2010, when he returned to Chairmanship, he worked at his home office when telecommuting was extremely rare in Korea. Samsung executives came to his home for meetings and briefings. According to a former Samsung executive who attended meetings at his home, KH liked to sit in a large sofa instead of sitting on a chair, so that he could observe people from different angles. It was reported that during a business trip, his hotel room was arranged like his room at home. When a foreign visitor suggested that he should run for a political office, KH replied, "I spend more time in pajamas, so I don't think it's possible to be a politician." But he certainly knew how to read people better than most politicians.

## CHAPTER 23

# Like Father, Like Son:
# Reading the Times

"**L**ike a pathfinder, he could absorb information, sniff the winds and sense what lies ahead," Walter Isaacson wrote about the late Steve Jobs in his biography. The same thing could be said about KH. If studying people was his main goal during school years, "getting a reading of the times" has been his preoccupation as a CEO. Those who knew his father commented on KH, "If father (BC) was a river, son (KH) is a sea." When BC summoned his lieutenants, they could guess what he was going to ask, but for KH, they didn't have a clue. They didn't have any idea which topic KH would discuss and how he would lead a dialogue. He was like a Zen master.

Once he asked the President of Shinsegye Department Store (which used to belong to the Samsung Group, but now is separated from the Group and run by the family of KH's sister), "What do you think are the characteristics of a department store business?" When the President couldn't answer, he answered for him:

> *"A department store is a real estate [not retail] business. The hotel business is a furnishing business rather than a service business. Semiconductor is a timing business. A watch belongs to the fashion business."*

Interestingly, Ray Kroc, McDonald's founder, once said that he was in the real estate business.

KH knew how to read the trends. In his essay published in 1997, KH stated: "Automobiles are electronics products... the boundaries between industries become meaningless." The 2014 International Consumer Electronics Show (CES) in Las Vegas must not have surprised KH when it featured a record number of automotive exhibitors. As KH predicted almost 20 years ago, the industry boundary between electronics and automotive is being blurred. He also pointed out that the service sector would become a more dominant player than manufacturing.

According to Wook Sohn, a former head of Samsung Talent Development Academy who worked at Samsung for 40 years and now teaches at Seoul National University in Korea, KH's insight comes from asking "why" to a question at least five times. In order to read the times well, KH said, a leader must ask:

- Why am I in this business?
- What are the fundamental goals for my business?
- What are the core technologies, products, characteristics, and distribution models?

Then, a leader needs to study the changes in external conditions, such as rules and regulations, technology development, and consumer attitudes. KH preferred seeing the forest first before seeing the trees.

Reading must have enhanced KH's "sense-making," which enabled him to interpret developments in the global business environment. Using the above framework, KH was able to read the present to predict the future and achieve higher goals. When Korea's GNP was $10,000 per capita, KH talked about what Korea needed to do to achieve $20,000 per capita. He emphasized the need for Korea to benchmark small, but strong countries. When Korea reached that goal, KH must have thought about how to reach $30,000 per capita with his continuous reading of the times. Like his father, BC was a voracious reader: On international flights, he read every single word from the front page to the last page of a newspaper. Interestingly, Bill Gates is also known for reading a magazine from cover to cover. "There's a universe in a book," said an influential Korean publisher. Through reading and reflection, successful people know how to align themselves to the timing of the universe.

.

## CHAPTER 24

# Think 3D

Thinking matters. The common theme of great companies is to think. "Think" was an IBM motto. "Think Fast" might be the new IBM motto, as its CEO Virginia Rometty told her employees. If "Think Different" was an Apple motto, "Think 3D" could be a Samsung motto. While some think that modern life is too hectic for thinking, the Rodin Museum in Paris has a long line of people who want to see its most famous collection, *The Thinker*. Successful people do take time to think. The Chinese character for thinking consists of two radicals—one, meaning field and the other, mind. Thinking cultivates a mind like a farmer cultivates a field.

Bill Gates, founder of Microsoft, is known for his annual "Think Week," but almost every week was a Think Week for KH. Some people say he was addicted to thinking, and he admitted that he had frequently thought five to ten years ahead. His way of thinking was not ordinary. KH was already thinking 3D before there was any talk of a 3D TV or glasses. How was KH able to develop three-dimensional thinking? During his Japanese school years, he was deep into movies to cope with loneliness. Some Sundays, he started watching movies from early morning to late night and was able to finish five or six movies. For two years, he watched more than 1,000 films. He said,

> *"After 100-200 movies, I was able to predict the plot of a movie. And after a while, I could clearly read the director's mind, a cameraman's position and the actor's attitude. In fact, while I was watching a film, I often put myself into the roles of the director, actor, cameramen and light technicians and could empathize with them. I frequently imagined my roles, switching from a director to an actor, from a cameraman to a lighting technician. I thought over how things could have been*

> *handled differently. As a result, I not only enjoyed watching a movie,*
> *but developed competencies almost like a film-making expert."*

To the question "What is management?" KH answered, "Seeing what is invisible." Watching a movie was a great learning experience, because it helped him think three-dimensionally beyond what he could see. "One can't solve a problem with the same thinking that created the problem," said Albert Einstein. KH appreciated different perspectives for creative solutions.

## CHAPTER 25

# Benchmark Small, but Strong Countries

While BC closely followed and benchmarked Japan, KH expanded the countries and companies for benchmarking. As Samsung recruited more Korean executives and technologists with U.S. higher education and work experience, it was natural that they brought some of the perspectives from their previous employers such as IBM, HP, Intel, Bell Labs, etc.

KH was particularly interested in small, but strong countries such as Finland, Switzerland and the Netherlands. During one of his executive meetings in Europe, he ordered Samsung's top Korean leaders to tour those countries to discover their strengths. Because Korea is a small country without many natural resources, he thought they might offer practices that Korea could adopt.

To accelerate a creative economy in Korea and to build an innovative culture at Samsung, Samsung recently produced a three-part webcast series entitled "Samsung Asks Israel about Creativity" for its employees. It was based on the research of Samsung's benchmarking study group who visited Israel to learn about its creative and innovation power. Israel has enjoyed great entrepreneurial success, with 64 Israeli companies listed on Nasdaq compared to nine Korean companies.

KH looked for inspiration from great companies as well. He ordered Samsung Economic Research Institute (SERI)—Samsung's Think Tank—to study GE's best practices and Jack Welch's leadership. GE's No. 1, speed, and Six Sigma initiatives became KH's mantra. Interestingly, former Samsung executive Myung-Woo Lee, Ph.D. revealed that GE had sent a delegation to Korea to study Samsung in 1996. When very few global leaders paid attention to Samsung, Jack Welch, then CEO of GE, noticed Samsung's growth potential and told GE executives to find out what GE could learn from Samsung. GE delegates were impressed with Samsung executives' and employees' commitment to organization, on-the-spot responsiveness to field issues, and speed in operations.

Since 1999, Samsung has been hosting an annual "advanced products exhibit' to help its executives and staff to assess the status quo of Samsung products in comparison with others. For example, the 12-day exhibit in 2007 displayed Samsung products with Sony, Panasonic, Sharp, GE, Nokia and Apple products side by side. Now the exhibit has been expanded and upgraded as "Samsung Innovation Forum." In 2012, Samsung looked back on their journey of product development and growth. These are opportunities for inspiration and an endless quest toward the best in class.

> *"In the Olympics 100 meter track event, there is only 0.01 second difference between the gold medal and the silver medal. That 0.01 second difference makes one athlete a hero and the other a person forgotten.... We have to accept the huge difference between the companies that make the premium brands and those who make ordinary products."*
>
> — KH Lee

## CHAPTER 26

# Lead like Ben-Hur

While BC paid attention to details in managing Samsung, KH painted a big picture and set strategic directions. Leaving tactical issues to professional managers, KH adopted a more humanistic approach toward executive rewards and promotions. He believed that incentives were one of the best inventions, so he didn't always punish the people who made mistakes and delivered poor results. "I have seen many failures caused by one's pride from small successes. I believe that people with a challenging spirit without fear of failure would enrich an organization more than ordinary people who are satisfied with small successes," said KH. Thus, he supported risk takers and even rewarded them for failures that could be justified.

His "more carrot, less carrot" approach, rather than carrot and stick, was inspired by his favorite movie *Ben-Hur*. He must have watched the movie hundreds of times from many different angles. Ben-Hur's horses won the race over Messala's because they were caressed, rather than whipped. KH noticed the difference between a first class horse trainer and a second class: how they motivated their horses.

BC talked against layoffs even in tough times, because it would lower employee morale. Comparing a workforce reduction to a red card in a soccer game, he argued:

> "A referee uses a yellow card on occasion, but avoids giving a red card, because it will break a game's flow and may affect a player's career. If that's the case for a 90-min. soccer game, an enduring company that will have to last tens or hundreds of years must avoid layoffs."

While BC told his staff to be cautious, KH's mantra was: "Don't worry about tapping (to make sure it's safe) before crossing a stone bridge. Even a wooden bridge, cross it first." He said,

> *"Profit is not the only thing that's measured. I give an A to a President who has posted a loss because he has made the necessary technology investment. But I would give a B or C to a leader who has achieved profit without any investment [for the future]."*

Unlike his father who never hired back any Samsung executive who had left Samsung, KH also brought back former Samsung executives who had joined other companies. Jong-Yong Yoon, former CEO of Samsung Electronics, resigned from Samsung to join Phillips and later joined Hyundai. But he was hired back and led SEC all the way to the top until May 2008. Some people believe that such a practice created a sense of alertness among Samsung executives and helped Samsung to know and learn from other companies' practices. It also prevented ex-Samsung executives from criticizing Samsung after their retirement from Samsung.

Former Samsung executives also credit KH's "detached involvement" for his success. He had keen eyes to pick the right leaders for the right positions. Those leaders were given autonomy to implement Samsung's vision and deliver operational excellence. KH didn't involve himself in daily management decisions, but he knew how to inspire them with critical questions, such as "Why is Sony a leader in technology?" He didn't provide how to be number one. One insightful question that he asked quite often enabled Samsung executives to find strategies to beat the competition. KH was able to achieve more by doing less.

With his bold spirit, KH challenged Samsung employees to trust and follow him. Promising "I will pay your salary out of my own pocket if the change doesn't work," he demanded loyal followership from his upper-echelon executives and employees.

## CHAPTER 27

# Apply the Lessons from Golf, Rugby and Baseball

**K**H was a sports maniac. In fact, it was reported that KH had regained consciousness after staying in a coma for two weeks when the Samsung Lions (the name of Samsung's baseball team in Korea) slugger hit a homerun in a baseball game in May 2014. Some of his family members who were watching the game in his ward saw him suddenly opening his eyes upon the cheerful noise of homerun. In high school, he was a wrestling champion. His skills in golf, table tennis and horse riding were above an amateur level. As a sportsman himself, he had a deep appreciation for the spirit of sports, sports marketing and athletes. In addition to serving as a member of the International Olympic Committee (IOC) since 1996, he has served on many different sports federation boards.

KH believed that playing sports was similar to running a business. Both require fair play, collaboration and sacrifice. During a meeting with Samsung Presidents at his home, KH shared his philosophy on sports: "It's easy for a golfer to hit 180 yards. With some coaching, 200 yards is possible and maybe hitting 230 yards will be within reach with more practice. However, if one wants to hit over 250 yards, he has to change everything, including stance and grip."

Since he enjoyed many sports, he emphasized sportsmanship to Samsung employees and told them to adopt the following lessons from three sports:

- Golf: rules, etiquette, autonomy, and self-discipline
- Baseball: supports a star pitcher and the spirit of a catcher who quietly works hard
- Rugby: strong will, mental toughness and unity.

> *"Golf is the only sport without a referee. That requires self-ruling and integrity. Baseball requires a combination of self-management and direction from a coach. Corporations need both star pitchers and catchers. Rugby builds endurance, especially under extreme conditions."*
>
> — KH Lee

KH also instilled sportsmanship to his children and encouraged JY to practice sports for wellness and management lessons. JY inherited his father's love for sports and played on the Korean national team for horseback riding during his college years. As an avid baseball fan, JY frequently attends sports games with his son. As a member of the Royal & Ancient Golf Club of St. Andrews and with a single-digit handicap, JY is known for his exceptional golf etiquette and consideration for other players on the course. He must have learned golf manners from his father and grandfather. BC had a reputation for impeccable manners and avoided playing a round with those who had bad manners. For example, he refused to play with anyone who cheated on his scores, didn't keep time, or screamed in the field. BC arrived for a round earlier than other players and didn't do a practice swing in a tee box because he didn't want to make others wait for him. The Lee family takes sports seriously and knows how to apply their love of sports for leading and marketing Samsung.

Samsung owns many professional sports teams, including its own baseball team and soccer team. It also sponsors the Manchester United soccer team and numerous local sports teams and events across the globe. Samsung has an annual CEO Cup that fosters employee competition within the Samsung League. Sportsmanship is a part of Samsung life.

## CHAPTER 28

# It's a Crime to Manufacture Products with Defects

"What's the difference between a $100,000 bonsai tree and a $10 bonsai tree?" KH asked Samsung's senior officials. He envisioned Samsung products to become superior brands that can demand premium prices. As early as 1993, he requested that each Samsung enterprise would produce one premium brand product.

Like his father, KH liked well-made products, and he was obsessed with quality. With his fine taste for first-class products, he was a trendsetter. The luxury wine served for his birthday party was sold as "Lee, Kun-Hee Wine" and his diet was called "the Emperor's diet" in Korea. Some people say that his obsession with premium brand names led Samsung to acquire several famous global brands, which weren't successful in the end.

When KH felt compelled to transform Samsung into a quality- first company, changing the mindset of professional managers was not easy even for an owner-CEO. KH told them that he would be willing to accept a decrease in market share or even shutting down operations for a year in order to achieve "0% quantity, 100% quality." As the story goes, one of his staff represented other executives' opinions and responded to KH, "We can't give up on quantity yet. Quality and quantity are two sides of a coin." KH got so angry at his comment that he threw a teaspoon on the table and walked away.

Having stated, "It is a crime to manufacture products with defects," KH demonstrated what he meant. In 1995, he had 150,000 phones with defects burned in front of 2,000 Samsung leaders and employees. The fire was meant as a departure from the past. One VP recollected the time: "I felt a thousand different feelings when I saw the ashes of the products that I worked on with my heart and soul." Those phones were worth over 5% of SEC's profit that year. KH also introduced a new rule to stop the production line when a defect was found. These extreme measures brought radical results for the Samsung Telecom operation.

It was not surprising that 600,000 Galaxy S3 pebble blue covers were destroyed nine days before the official release date of the phone in 2012. They didn't look as good as originally intended. "The Galaxy effect" on SEC's record revenues and profits wasn't an easy victory for those involved in making the phones. It was a prize won through their fanatic obsession with quality for over 20 years. Now that Samsung's focus on quality has been achieved, some believe that innovation and service should be its next focus.

---

## QUALITY MATTERS:
## TWO LEATHER SHOES MAKERS

A long, long time ago, there were two leather shoemakers with the family names of Kim and Park in a Korean village. Kim was rich, while Park didn't even have enough food to feed his family. The reason was that Kim made lots of shoes and sold them at a low price because their quality was low. But Park didn't have many shoes to sell, because he was putting his heart and soul to make the best quality shoes. Due to his intense labor, Park's shoes were much more expensive. One day, their village leader ordered from each of them a pair of leather shoes to be presented to the King. The king loved Park's shoes and requested that several pairs be sent every year. Soon Park became famous throughout the country as the King's shoemaker. As the orders were coming from all over the place, Park had to train apprentices and hire other craftsmen. Now the fortunes of Kim and Park were reversed: Park became rich, while Kim became very poor.

— A story appeared in KH's essay on quality

## CHAPTER 29

# Master the Art
# of Communication

R alph Waldo Emerson said, "What you do speaks so loudly that I can't hear what you are saying." For most people in Korea, KH was the message. Nobody will deny his charisma from within. It's not soft charisma, but since he doesn't talk much, when he opens his mouth, everyone listens. KH was not a smooth talker, but he was an effective communicator. He was a storyteller. To make a point, he used analogies and often drew lessons from nature—fish, flowers, animals, etc. He could be called the Gaudi of management because Spanish architect Antoni Gaudi drew inspiration for his architecture from nature and designed such masterpieces as the Sagrada Familia in Barcelona, Spain.

KH's mastery of public communication was not an accident. He started his Samsung career at TBS, a broadcasting station that used to be owned by Samsung before he became the Vice Chairman of the Samsung Group. With its media-savvy Chairman, Samsung uses an internal cable TV station (SBC) and social media for the CEO's messages and major company announcements. SBC even has employee correspondents who report from Samsung's various locations and share the news of their regional sites.

To disseminate KH's message for Samsung's New Management 1.0 in 1993, Samsung hired a famous author and created a comic book. As serious as his intention was, KH wanted to be able to reach his audience in a user-friendly way. At the same time, he also knew how to use shock therapy, such as changing the work hours of all employees, to communicate with impact. In order to bring on megachange, he had to change their habits. The message did stick in the minds of Samsung men. In a speech in early 2013, Keun-Hee Park, Vice Chairman of Samsung Life Insurance, said, "The memory of New Management in 1993 is still vivid even 20 years later. If we study its theme and execute the Chairman's will again, Samsung will be able to find another vision for the next 100 years."

For efficient internal communication, KH also directed a book *The Language of Samsung*, which compiled the terms and phrases that Samsung people must understand. The following stories are two examples in the book.

---

## THE GOOSE THEORY

Geese fly in formation. The leader goose flies in front and the rest will follow him. Even at night, they don't get lost, as long as the leading goose knows where it's going. This is equivalent to the fugleman in a military formation, a political movement or a company leadership team.

---

## THE FROG THEORY

Frogs have eyes on their heads. They were created or evolved to be able to see with a nearly 360-degree perspective for survival. Humans don't have such a keen sensitivity to an upcoming crisis as animals do.

---

## CHAPTER 30

# Pave the Road for Successors

In Jan. 2014, KH turned 72. He has survived cancer, and has been in the hospital after a heart attack in May 2014. No one mentions his official retirement, although some people speculate that JY will lead Samsung by 2015. Like his father, KH has orchestrated successful succession planning. In Dec. 2012, his only son Jae-Yong Lee (JY) was promoted to Vice Chairman of SEC with a reorganization that would ensure a smooth transition of power to him. Earlier, KH's staff was convicted of various illegal transactions to give JY control over the Samsung Group. For his knowledge of the transactions, KH was sentenced to three years in jail, but he never served the sentence. Some Koreans question the legitimacy of JY's inherited leadership position; however, unless there is a major blunder by Samsung or JY, he is on the road to reign in the Samsung Kingdom. Samsung Group has been making efforts to increase JY's control of Samsung Group through various changes in its holding structure. JY has also shown more active roles in strategic decisions since his father's hospitalization. KH's first daughter, nicknamed Little KH, runs the Shilla Hotel (a luxury Korean hotel brand), and the other daughter is a president at Everland and Cheil Worldwide, an advertising and public relations company.

JY, also known as Jay, has been taking management lessons since childhood. Koreans emphasize the importance of education at their family dining tables. Parents' wisdom is passed on to children by osmosis during meals. KH reportedly instructed JY to read the business and economy sections of daily newspapers since his middle-school days. JY has completed elite courses for any Korean leader. He studied Eastern history at the prestigious Seoul National University in Korea, and then received an MBA from Japan's elite Keio University. Then he enrolled in the Ph.D. program at Harvard Business School. His father recommended studying in Japan first before going to the USA, so that he could appreciate the power of details (small is beautiful in Japan) before he experienced the grand scale of the U.S.

When JY became an executive at Samsung in 2001, KH requested that JY travel to all global sites, build personal networks, and play golf with top Samsung executives on Saturdays. When he was promoted to Vice President, KH gave him a painting that depicted a story from *Three Kingdoms*, a Chinese classic. The story was a reminder of the importance of hiring top talent: If you see a great talent, humble yourself and ask him or her to join Samsung and work with him/her patiently.

JY had mentors inside and outside of Samsung. He attended GE's senior executive program. Fluent in Japanese and English, he has built wide global networks, from Chinese political leaders to European business leaders. He was the only Asian executive who was invited to attend the late Apple CEO Steve Jobs' funeral.

In order to benchmark family business succession planning, KH visited the Wallenbergs, a prominent Swedish family known for bankers, industrialists, politicians, diplomats and philanthropists. Among the more celebrated of the Wallenbergs is Raoul Wallenberg who rescued tens of thousands of Jews in Nazi-occupied Hungary during World War II while he served as a special envoy in Budapest and issued protective passports for Jews. The Wallenbergs' business empire is a large group of companies that has lasted for several generations. The Wallenbergs keep a very low-key public profile and avoid conspicuous displays of wealth with the family motto *"Esse non Videri"* (Latin for "To be, not to be seen").

Even with such preparation, KH can't be so confident of the future for Samsung under his son. A Korean saying goes, "There's no rich family whose wealth has lasted three generations." JY will be the third generation. A Korean journalist assessed that JY's battle to win in the global marketplace would be a tough one because he will have to face the first generation [talented and spirited] Chinese entrepreneurs such as the founders of Alibaba, Tencent, Baidu and Xiaomi. His grandfather BC also wrote, "Starting a new enterprise is difficult. But keeping [growing] an established business is even more difficult." It must be a tremendous burden for JY to inherit Samsung at its highest point and attempt to repeat a God-sized CEO's legacy.

# IV

# The Samsung Empire

## CHAPTER 31

# The Republic or Kingdom of Samsung?

South Korea's official name is the Republic of Korea (ROK). It has been the 6th Republic since 1988, when Korea elected a former military leader as President, but some people think Korea has become the Republic of Samsung during the reign of civilian Presidents. They deplore that Samsung has become so powerful that even the government can't handle it. Some Koreans even wonder if the Samsung Chairman has more power than the President of Korea. While most CEOs of large conglomerates attended the inauguration ceremony of its first female President Geun-Hey Park, KH skipped it, citing that he was in Hawaii for health reasons.

If Samsung were compared to a country, it wouldn't be the USA or the UK. It wouldn't be quite like certain kingdoms or nations where subjects can't criticize their kings or governments. Nevertheless, KH was often called "the emperor" with absolute power and control. A former SEC Chief Legal Counsel wrote in his book *Think Samsung*, "Samsung Presidents pledged loyalty to KH and executives wouldn't have liquids before their meeting with KH. KH didn't go to the restroom during meetings, so they didn't feel comfortable about doing that." A former Samsung executive observed that even senior Samsung leaders would bow low to KH's children to show utmost respect to "the royal family." JY, in his 40s, is known for being more informal than KH, however, it is unknown how his brand of "smart leadership" will implement an egalitarian approach.

SEC's sales have contributed to 16.5% of Korea's GDP in 2012. If the whole Samsung group is counted, it will be nearly a quarter of Korea's GDP. Interestingly, foreign ownership of SEC shareholders has been varying from 47% to 60% and over 60% of its 240,000 global employees are non-Koreans.

Unlike Sony, which tried a foreign Board of Directors and British CEO Sir Howard Stringer, the Samsung board remains Korean. Samsung's Board of Directors consisted entirely of Korean males over 55, but in 2013 they elected a female university professor on the Board. It is worth noting that its main competitor, Apple, also had an all American Board of Directors with two female members as of August 2014. In 2013, Toyota tapped a former executive from its U.S. rival—General Motors—to join its board. For the first time since its founding in 1937, Toyota appointed a director from outside the company. It will be interesting to see whether Samsung will follow suit in the global diversity of its Board.

## CHAPTER 32

# Balance of Executive Power
# and Influence

Despite a perception that KH made all of the important decisions, he delegated a lot of responsibilities to professional managers. He decided on key management themes, such as developing world-class products or genius management, but he relied on the Office of Future Strategy to implement the theme.

A former executive revealed that KH had discussed important issues with his leadership team and that the discussions had often lasted till 2:00 AM or 3:00 AM. The Office of Future Strategy, which used to be a part of the almighty Chairman's Office during the BC era, has gone through several name changes that reflected the times. During the IMF crisis, it was called the Restructuring Committee. Although their power and influence has varied, it's still considered to be the most powerful office and often called the "Control Tower." With over 150 brains under six teams including strategy, management audit, communication, compliance and human resources, the Office has been led by Samsung Group Vice Chairman Gee-Sung Choi. In 2014, KH reshuffled the office, transferring key leaders to SEC and replacing them with younger executives from SEC. Some interpreted that this reorganization will strengthen the authority of SEC which is already the most powerful group within Samsung due to its overwhelming contribution to Samsung's revenue.

With full authority from the Board of Directors, the Office can make key decisions and coordinate enterprise activities after consulting other Samsung executives and outside experts. Additionally, all Samsung group Presidents attend a "Wednesday Presidents' Meeting" which has been held since the BC days. They meet every Wednesday morning, listen to lectures on various topics and discuss ideas. Reportedly, leadership has been one of the most popular topics at the meeting. A critical number of executives at the top have spent their entire career at Samsung so many can read each other's minds through their shared experience. They also have a lot of autonomy in managing their own platforms.

Most Korean companies make announcements for executive level promotions at the end or the beginning of a year. Samsung executives often don't have any idea about their fate until the night before. They may speculate about their moves, but they are kept in the dark until the last moment. Executives with the titles of VPs and above seldom leave Samsung voluntarily.

Another key facilitator for Samsung's strategic decisions is the Samsung Economic Research Institute (SERI), a powerful think tank with its own publishing arm. In collaboration with the Office, they draw a strategic roadmap for Samsung and its affiliates. Presidents execute plans based on it. SERI conducts research, publishes books and white papers, and holds seminars on global trends, domestic trends, industries, consumer behaviors, leadership and many other areas. SERI's research is so cutting edge that it even influences the Korean government's policy makers.

## CHAPTER 33

# Images of Samsung
# and "Samsung Men"

Many Koreans seem to have love-hate relationships with Samsung. When they go abroad, they are proud of Samsung logos visible all over the place, from the airport luggage carts to the TVs in the hotel rooms. Most of them would acknowledge that Samsung has improved the Korea Inc. brand. But a lot of Koreans also believe that Samsung has become too arrogant, aggressive and ruthless. Despite the public's mixed feelings about Samsung, Samsung Korea is still the most favorite employer for college graduates and attracts more than 100,000 applicants for about 4,000 new college graduate positions per hiring season (twice a year). It is not uncommon that applicants take private lessons or tutoring to prepare for the Global Samsung Aptitude Test (GSAT) and interviews. Some applicants are reportedly considering plastic surgeries to create a so-called "Samsung-type face," which is known as the preferred look by Samsung interviewers. The entrance exam for Samsung is so competitive that it is often compared to the prestigious "bar exam" and "civil service exams" for Korean lawyers and public officials. Samsung employees enjoy the prestige, benefits and compensation. The findings of a 2012 survey of young Koreans' perceptions of Samsung employees included the following terms: young male (age 30-34), intelligent, technical, formal, authoritarian, urban, and trendy.

Does Samsung's image fare better overseas? Having worked with Samsung's diverse global stakeholders—employees, customers, partners and suppliers—for over 20 years, I can say that foreign perceptions of Samsung vary depending on their nature of interactions with the company. Although they are different from country to country and from one business unit to another, the most frequently cited perceptions are the following:

- A global company that plays hardball
- A very well-organized company
- A very demanding company with extremely hard-working people and a shared goal
- Paranoid
- Efficient
- Huge, vertically integrated
- Successful
- Desirable as a customer (because of high volume)
- Prefer Korean suppliers and in-house development
- Manipulative
- Borrow intellectual property
- Demanding
- Micromanaging
- Top-down
- Don't have the best reputation in the industry.

Below are comments from Samsung global employees and partners:

*"Prior to working with Koreans, I had heard that they were among the most friendly and outgoing of the Asian community. However, after interacting with Samsung people as customers, my impressions have changed. They appear very secretive and seem to regard non-Koreans as untrustworthy. Americans seem to be a necessary evil to them."*

*"It's hard to work with Samsung as a partner. They share very little information for us to work together. Samsung employees have sometimes been arrogant and demanding while offering very little positive reinforcement."*

*"Samsung often has the 'my way or the highway' mentality. They ask for everything, but don't want to give anything."*

*"Samsung is a very capable, worldwide industrial powerhouse that wants to dominate every market in which they conduct business."*

*"Samsung has unrealistic expectations of timelines and manpower allocation."*

*"One must be tough to work at Samsung."*

*"We experience the obvious difficulties in communication whenever we meet with Samsung dispatchers who are used to the ways of working in Korea. I get the impression that they are accustomed to being the dominating force in Korea, and are not able to grasp the 'cooperative teaming' arrangement that we are used to here in the U.S."*

*"Samsung people strive to meet and exceed high goals. They expect dedication and commitment from their employees and vendor support. They treat their employees well and reward them when goals are achieved."*

## CHAPTER 34

# Samsung Citizen's Life: From Cradle to Grave

S amsung dominates the lives of Korean citizens, especially Samsung men, from the cradle to the grave. Let's track the life and career of a hypothetical Korean businessman KJ Park who joins Samsung after college.

He starts his workday watching Samsung internal cable news.

After three years of working at Samsung, KJ finds the woman of his dreams and is thinking about getting married.

Through Samsung's intranet, he schedules a meeting with a wedding planner who provides details of options for his wedding. (Working at Samsung, he won't have much time to prepare for a wedding himself.) He joyfully holds a wedding ceremony at an event hall in the Samsung Headquarters building in Seoul.

He spends the first night with his bride at the Shilla Hotel (owned by Samsung) before he travels to Thailand for his honeymoon the next day.

He buys luxury brand cosmetics for his wife at the Shilla Duty Free Shop at the Incheon Airport. These are all charged on his Samsung Visa Card.

During the honeymoon, he and his wife call their parents using a Samsung Galaxy phone.

They move into a condominium built by Samsung Engineering and Construction. It is equipped with a Samsung refrigerator, a Samsung washer and a Samsung air-conditioner.

His wife is pregnant and two days before the due date, she checks into the Samsung Medical Center with the most advanced facilities and equipment.

With a new addition to the family, the couple gets Samsung Life Insurance.

The family visits a Theme Park called Samsung Everland.

His boy becomes a fan of the Samsung Giants, a baseball team.

For college, he considers applying for Sungkyoonkwan University owned by Samsung Group.

KJ moves up the corporate ladder, becomes an executive and starts playing golf at the Benest Country Club (one of five golf courses owned by Samsung).

He gets old and he looks for a Samsung nursing home.

Of course, when he is dead, there is a morgue at the Samsung hospital.

## CHAPTER 35

# Pledge of Allegiance:
# Company First!

One of my "Doing Business with Korea" workshop attendees in the U.S. wrote about his perception of Korea:

> *"Koreans have a country-first/company-second/individual-third mentality."*

According to CEO Score, a Korean organization that assesses corporate management performance, the average tenure for employees working at 169 companies of Korea's 30 largest conglomerates was only 9.7 years in 2013. The average for Samsung employees was 9.34 years.

Although the number looks similar to other companies, loyalty to the company among those who stay at Samsung may be exceptional. Working for the most prestigious group in Korea, Samsung men and women are proud to be Samsung citizens. Some seem to believe that Samsung (especially SEC) is the best company to work for and that Samsung products are the best, at least in Korea. They would not mind lifelong employment at Samsung for job security and prestige, if possible. It is said that Samsung men's blood color turns to blue (the color of Samsung's logo) during their new hire orientation. Executives who live and breathe Samsung are Samsung men to the bone, to their inner core.

The majority of Samsung Korean employees don't leave it voluntarily. At Samsung Korea, the turnover rate in 2011 was 5%, whereas the rate at overseas operations was 15.6%. In Korea, it becomes news when a Samsung employee leaves the company and pursues other interests. A Korean manager on an expat assignment at a Samsung's U.S. subsidiary couldn't understand how Americans could quit a prestigious employer like Samsung. With excellent benefits and compensation, Samsung employees can enjoy a comfortable standard of living. Thus, unlike other Korean companies, labor unions are not active at Samsung. It was BC's idea to disallow unions; however, he wanted to take care of employees' welfare, including their family's healthcare and children's education.

It seems that some Samsung employees put the company first, even before the laws and their own interests. For several years since 2005, Korea's Fair Trade Commission wanted to audit SEC for potentially illegal activities. Reportedly, several employees destroyed documents or erased hard disks to eliminate any evidence. Knowing that they could be criminally charged for such behaviors, were they willing to sacrifice themselves to protect Samsung?

Kazuo Inamori, founder of Kyocera and CEO of Japan Airlines, wrote in his book, *A Passion for Success*:

> *"As executives, we should maintain a value system in which we automatically place our company's benefit first... When faced with the choice of benefiting self or the group, it is the basic moral obligation of a leader—always and without any hesitation—to place the group's interest ahead of his or her own."*

He probably did not mean compromising personal integrity for a company's interest.

Some people point out that Samsung employees are loyal, but don't necessarily love the company. Hyundai outdoes Samsung in employees' love for the company and bonding among them. Younger generations are more likely to pursue what they love rather than seek job security. One former employee wrote a book entitled, *I Like My Life More than Samsung*. Yet he is in the minority. Samsung employees and executives rarely complain about the company in public.

# BC LEE VS. PROSECUTOR

It was during the 2nd Republic of Korea after the military coup of Apr. 19th in 1960. The government wanted to eliminate the people who illegally accumulated wealth. So many corporations were being investigated and Samsung was one of them. The prosecutor summoned Samsung managers, directors, Vice Presidents, Senior Vice Presidents and finally the CEO, BC. The prosecutor asked BC, "Every single Samsung manager I have interviewed says that he is the person responsible for tax evasion. Who do you really think is the person for that responsibility?"

BC replied, "It's not even a question. Since they followed the order of the CEO, I'm the one who is responsible for that." The prosecutor was impressed with BC's answer. "It was only in Samsung that everyone wanted to take responsibility for the problem."

BC was encouraged by the prosecutor's comment and asked him: "By the way, who is the one that made it impossible to do business in Korea without tax evasion?" And BC listed the reasons why tax evasion was inevitable. Corporate tax was 35% and business income tax was 15%. The taxes were astronomically high and all Samsung's profits wouldn't be enough to cover them. The prosecutor was speechless.

## CHAPTER 36

# Samsung Constitution

The official name of the Constitution written by KH is *Samsung Management Principle*. He set "the recovery of moral values" as the number one priority of Samsung and emphasized humanity, integrity, protocol and etiquette as its core values. His mandates include:

- Comply with the laws and ethical standards.
- Maintain a clean organizational culture.
- Respect customers, shareholders and employees.
- Care for the environment, health and safety.
- Be a socially responsible citizen.

The new hires of Samsung learn these principles with details. Specific behaviors are reinforced during the orientation programs of newly promoted executives.

Like most corporate core values, these are only ideals, so there have been violations at Samsung. After an internal audit in 2001, Samsung reprimanded 50 executives and employees for taking bribes and receiving entertainment from suppliers. Many suppliers got warnings, but some were permanently banned from doing business with Samsung.

In 2013, Samsung voluntarily returned a certificate that it had received for being a pro-environment group. It was a token of apology for the death of a supplier's employee during the repair of a toxic chemical leak at a Samsung facility.

It is worth noting KH's emphasis on humanity in Samsung's Management Principles. Unlike the legalistic tendencies of many Western countries, many Asians still believe that the laws are made for humans, not the other way around. Justice without mercy is still not always accepted in Asia. KH said, "An organization lacking humanity and integrity can't become a world-class company. I won't be happy if Samsung has $1 of profit without them."

For KH, humanity is not about being "nice" to people who need corrections. A leader with humanity will guide them to the right path with a sincere desire to help them to stretch and grow. That is real humanity at Samsung. KH also believed that "good manners are essential for global humanity."

## CHAPTER 37

# Do You Speak Samsung?

According to a Center for Creative Leadership newsletter, "A change in business strategy demands a change of leadership culture—and a shift in language, too."

With his New Management initiative, KH ordered his team to create a Samsung Phrases Book. The goals of the publication were to:

- Clarify the language.
- Create unique Samsung phrases.
- Elevate them to a higher level (concise, but deep meaning to save time for communication and to facilitate comprehension within a few seconds).

The book consists of 113 short cases and stories that have messages for self-management and development. It states:

> *"The language of an organization is critical to uniting its members' thoughts and behaviors. It delivers the direction and values through words. Thus, it is necessary to unify the language for implementing our vision…taking Samsung to a first-class enterprise in the 21st century."*

KH believed that it would improve efficiency in internal communication if employees could have a conversation by just using a few phrases with a shared meaning. That common language was to increase unity among employees and improve effective communication. For example, every Samsung employee understands the meaning of "pulling a leg from the back." During the meeting in Frankfurt, Germany, KH said to his audience, "Out of 100 people, there are one or two people who hold another's leg from the back. For us to succeed, it is important to eliminate this 1-2% of people. If you want to run, run. If you want to walk fast, walk fast. If you don't even want to walk, play. I will guarantee your livelihood. I will pay your salary. Samsung will not kick you out. So [if you don't want to do anything,] stay still, instead of pulling someone's leg from the back. Why would you prevent a colleague from moving forward and make him go astray?"

The terms and definitions in Samsung phrases have shaped the process of Samsung's cultural change. In that book, there is a description of "comprehensive technologist." "A competent technologist must understand the core of his technology and follow its change and trends. He should avoid thinking 'I'm number one' and must be keenly aware of his strengths and weaknesses. In learning from technical advisors, he should not believe that he has gotten all the lessons when he has only limited knowledge. He must be open-minded instead of insisting on his views only. Today's technologists must always think from customers' perspectives and apply them to their work."

## THE BOEING 747 STRATEGY

There is a story of a Boeing 747 in "*Samsung Phrases.*" The plane will explode if it doesn't reach the level of 10,000 feet within a few minutes of takeoff. If it stops in the middle, it will crash. Samsung can't afford to stop in the middle of its ascent. Soon it may have to descend.... When and how, no one knows.... Samsung products could be wiped out from the face of the earth within 10 years. Like a Boeing jet that could go for the long haul, Samsung could enjoy the flights for another 30 years or 50 years, although some areas may be bumpy depending on external factors and the pilot who can manage the storm.

## CHAPTER 38

# Cluster Samsung Towns
# for Efficiency and Synergy

S amsung often shocks the world with its super-scale investments. The semiconductor and LCD businesses require large, time-sensitive investments to maintain competitiveness. When Samsung builds, they don't construct buildings. They build towns. In 2013 SEC opened the R5 research institute that comprises two 27-story towers and houses 10,000 employees within Samsung Digital City in Suwon, near Seoul. Designed to integrate the IT and mobile divisions for collaboration and innovation, it was an addition to the four other research institutes in that area and includes a space for co-working with suppliers.

"We have to maximize the limited land in Korea. If all executives and employees live in the same complex, they can gather within 40 seconds for a meeting. That's our competitiveness. We save logistics expenses and achieve management speed. That will eliminate traffic jams too. Let's construct buildings higher, not wider," said KH.

KH had a vision of building a 110-story Samsung "intelligent building" in the Gangnam district in Seoul, not too far from Samsung's Headquarters in Seocho-dong, but it didn't happen after the neighborhood protested. So on that land, Samsung built a luxury condominium complex called Tower Palace, in which many top Samsung executives reside. The more power they had at Samsung, the higher and the larger their units were.

"Scattered we die, gathered we live." KH applied the same concept to Samsung facility management for the efficiency of saving time and distribution costs. Samsung facilities around the world, whether in China, Vietnam or Mexico, are mega complexes. In fact, Samsung has built the world's largest mobile phone manufacturing facility in Vietnam where 130 million units are produced a year.

At Samsung, many functions are co-located in one building. Everybody can gather for a meeting in five minutes. If co-locating is not possible, Samsung enables regular gatherings for virtual and remote teams, since there is no substitute for face-to-face meetings for speedy decisions and execution. For example, a wireless team member in Suwon can use helicopters that run twice a day to see another team member in the plant in Gumi, in the southern part of Korea. In 30 minutes, they can have a team meeting. A portion of the R&D team is already in the plant.

According to a Korean newspaper, Toyota, during its recent recall crisis, studied organizations known for speedy decision-making, such as Samsung and Hyundai Motors. Toyota's conclusion was to enable a "one stop" process—from the conceptualization of an idea to a final decision—by putting all the teams necessary for a task in one building. That creates the power of convergence.

## CHAPTER 39

# Border Control and Security Solutions

S amsung's intelligence and security is so legendary in Korea that some believe Samsung's intelligence exceeds that of the Korean government. In April 2013, when the world speculated on a potential war between North Korea and South Korea due to the threat from the North, Korean Netizens (citizens on the Internet) commented that there would be no war because KH returned to Korea from a three-month trip. They reasoned that Samsung's intelligence would have recommended their Chief not to return home if a war had been imminent.

It is said that Samsung procurement teams know suppliers' margins and profitability in detail. Public relations teams may study influential journalists' backgrounds and traits. With that kind of in-house intelligence, Samsung is paranoid about its own security. Visiting Samsung seems to be stricter than going through any airport security. The lens of a visitor's camera phone is taped in black. If someone attempts to take it off, the lens will be damaged. Even at U.S. Samsung sites, I had to leave my camera phone and computer with a receptionist. I couldn't even take a USB stick for a presentation.

Many people believe that Samsung is watching its own employees too, at least in Korea. According to Yong-Chul Kim, former Chief Legal Counsel at Samsung, monitoring emails and wiretapping phone calls were a common practice at Samsung Korea.

It is reported that cameras are everywhere. Upon arrival, the uses of smartphone cameras, Bluetooth devices and memory accessories are prohibited. In fact, all executives and employees are required to use a Mobile Device Management (MDM) app, which blocks cameras attached to smartphones upon entering Samsung offices and facilities. Only a mobile phone's voice and text features are allowed. Once, I sent a needs assessment to some SEC employees, and their attached responses came back encrypted and unreadable. Former Samsung employees revealed that all the files created by employees were saved in the central server, and that they couldn't take any documents outside.

One employee mentioned that Samsung Korea's copier paper costs 20-30 cents per sheet because of embedded metal sensors. During business trips, employees don't open notebooks in public areas out of fear of losing confidentiality. Another Samsung insider said that Samsung didn't distribute hard copies of training materials to new hires. They worry that they will lose their intellectual property if some leave the company. Interestingly, Apple seems to share Samsung's secretive approach toward training programs. According to a *New York Times* article on Apple's internal training programs (August, 10, 2014), Apple employees are discouraged from talking about the company in general, including training classes; no pictures of the classrooms have surfaced publicly. At Samsung, security is reinforced through regular employee training.

## INFORMATION SECURITY TIPS FOR "SAMSUNG MEN"

- *Security is Samsung's lifeline.*
- *The basics of security are to follow the rules.*
- *Security is similar to an office love that an employee is about to start.*
- *Even a simple report on your desk could be confidential.*
- *Trust doesn't exist in security.*
- *Information leaked can't be recovered and will result in damage.*
- *For top-secret information, create your own code or symbol.*
- *At drinking venues, make sure that your hands are empty (don't take documents).*
- *Prevention is the best policy.*
- *Inform us of your location during a business trip.*

Source: *Learn from Enemies: Hyundai-Samsung Stealing from Each Other* by Young-Bae Ahn and Won-Bae Park

## CHAPTER 40

# Document and Share
# to Triple Sales

I once went to a presentation by Google representatives. Getting information internally is more difficult than getting it externally, said a presenter. If that were true for most companies, it would be similar for SEC. Thus, Samsung has been promoting "One Samsung" as many multinationals have done for a sense of unity. Almost 20 years ago when the Internet was not so widely used, Samsung had a goal to deliver the CEO's message to the manager level within 12 hours and a message from the lowest rank to the CEO within 24 hrs. Since 1999, Samsung has furthered its vision for information sharing and created "Single Samsung," a companywide resource management system for speed. It was a legacy from the founder who had the habit of documenting information and instilled the same habit to the employees.

The emphasis on documentation started from BC days. Known as a "memo-maniac", BC instilled the habit of documenting in his children and employees, and KH used to give fountain pens to newly promoted VPs to encourage the habit. He believed writing something down would increase memorization. The memo feature of the Galaxy Note may have its root in Samsung's corporate culture. KH deplored the lack of documentation in Korean pottery history and at the company:

> *"The reason why the craftsmanship of Korea's Koryo Dynasty (918-1392) celadon and Chosun Dynasty (1392-1910) celadon was not transferred was because of a lack of documentation. A first-class country is a country that teaches lessons from history through records so that nations, businesses and individuals will not repeat the same*

> *mistakes. We are wasting so much by not documenting. Executives in transition need to leave documents that can become a book containing their contacts, success stories and failures... Without those documents, we all suffer from continued disconnection."*

"If we can share information well, we can increase the sales revenue three times," KH declared. He emphasized horizontal and vertical sharing of documentation for effective communication that would overcome the barriers between departments and enterprises. He believed that well-kept records provide the source of creativity for quality management.

With such an emphasis on sharing records, it was not surprising to hear from a Samsung training team that they wanted to videotape my workshop. They said that they intended to share the program content with others who didn't get to attend. A Samsung manager told me that business trips are stressful not because of jet lag, but because of reports they have to submit after each trip. The reports become their co-learning resources. Samsung also encourages documenting failures. Some failures may not be avoidable in business; however, Samsung wants to prevent repeated mistakes by sharing the lessons from failures. They can often be used as case studies during executive leadership sessions.

KH emphasized documentation for personal and professional development as well. He encouraged professionals to keep records of their daily activities and to evaluate their time management one year later. Every January, he himself tallied his past year's activities, including the numbers of overseas trips, customer visits, management meetings, golf outings, etc. This simple analysis gave him a big picture for his new year's schedule. It is based on his conviction: "Whether it's a nation, corporation or individual, the first class seeks lessons from history with well-kept documents."

# V

# Samsung Inside

## CHAPTER 41

# Korean Culture vs. Samsung Culture

"Is this Korean culture or Samsung culture?" is one of the most frequently asked questions by the people who are working for or with Samsung. My answer is "It depends" on what "this" is.

Often it is both, but certainly there is a unique Samsung culture that is different from other Korean companies' corporate cultures. Corporate cultures are influenced by many factors, including the founder's education, philosophy, industry and management styles. Hyundai started its business in the construction industry and grew the enterprise in the heavy industries, so some see a more masculine energy and humanistic bonding at Hyundai. Some Koreans contrast Hyundai and Samsung like night and day, comparing different backgrounds, personalities and leadership styles of their founders and current leaders. One can easily notice their differences not only in decision-making and management styles, but also in employees' dating and drinking styles. Besides both Samsung and Hyundai have numerous subsidiaries in different industries. Even in the same semiconductor industry, both customers and suppliers recognize cultural differences between Samsung and SK Hynix. The latter was a merger between Hyundai Electronics and LG Semiconductor and in 2012 SK Group acquired a major stake in Hynix. So the history certainly shapes its corporate culture. A leader's management style also has a huge impact on the culture of a specific company or division.

Despite different corporate cultures, understanding core Korean values is still important to working with Samsung and other Korean companies. Multinationals that operate globally tend to carry the flags of their corporate headquarters. Thus IBM subsidiaries may have some characteristics of U.S. companies, Huawei may have a Chinese cultural influence, and Toshiba will certainly have some Japanese values.

According to *Cultural Detective South Korea* (www.culturaldetective.com), key Korean values include:

- *Een-gan-jeok*: humanistic
- *Woori*: we-ness
- Chae-myun: face
- *Seo-yeol*: hierarchy
- *Nun-chi*: ability to size up a situation without verbal communication
- *Geun-myun*: hard working ethic

In addition, one can observe the following concepts in Koreans:

- *Kkeun*: ties and connections that bind relationships
- *Jeong*: emotional bond
- *Kkang*: guts to take risk
- *Oghi*: a challenging spirit to prove naysayers wrong

Like most multinationals, Samsung strives to keep a balance between the corporate headquarters culture and the regional/local cultures. However, it will take a while for Samsung to achieve that balance, given its strong tendency to control at the Korean Headquarters.

## CHAPTER 42

# Fusion Leadership— East Meets West

A company's corporate culture is influenced by the background and management philosophy of its founder and the leaders who followed. Since Samsung Group had only two chairmen for over 75 years, their backgrounds have had powerful impacts on the group. BC was educated in Japan, spent part of each year in Japan, and benchmarked Japan in many businesses. Samsung was very similar to Japanese corporations during his reign. Since he and his staff were fluent in Japanese due to the Japanese colonization of Korea, Japan was a role model. In fact, some believe that even Samsung's group name reflected BC's admiration for Mitsui Group, a Japanese conglomerate. The first Chinese character for both Samsung and Mitsui is the same, meaning three. BC established similar businesses in which Mitsui was active. In addition, Sony was Samsung's benchmarking model for a long time, until Samsung became a model for Sony's benchmarking.

BC was also a student of Confucius, a Chinese philosopher from the 5th Century B.C., so his teaching became a model of his management principle. Both BC and KH applied the teachings of Chinese philosophers to their leadership and management.

However, KH was exposed to western culture through his graduate education in the USA. While Japan was his friend, teacher and competition, KH had a larger world of reference than his father. Also, as more Koreans received their graduate education in the U.S., they had more exposure to American business culture. The leaders who studied and worked in the USA brought some of the best practices from U.S. corporations, such as IBM, Intel, HP and GE. Interestingly, a former Samsung employee from Japan wrote that Samsung's success was a combination of Japanese technology and equipment and the U.S. management style.

Adopting the Western business system in Korea wasn't always easy; yet Samsung was able to build a hybrid style of the Japanese and Western management systems. Below are a few examples identified by Tarun Khanna, Jae-Yong Song, and Kyung-Mook Lee in a *Harvard Business Review* article, "The Paradox of Samsung's Rise:"

- *Strategy: Diversification but more focus within businesses*
- *Competition: Focus on continuous improvement and applied R&D but also on innovation, marketing, and design to establish brand and premium pricing*
- *Supplier relationship: Long-term cooperative supplier relationships but with some level of competition*
- *Recruitment: Interweaving of internal workforce while attracting outsiders through market-based compensation; annual recruitment for entry-level positions; ongoing recruitment for experienced hires*
- *Promotion and rewards: Coexistence of seniority-based and merit-based promotion and compensation; mostly standardized but some individualized incentives*

For Samsung, managing the different business values and polarities of East and West is not a matter of either/or, but a choice of both/and.

## CHAPTER 43

# Perpetual Crisis and Contingency Plan

When Apple announced its iPhone sales in Korea in Nov. 2009, Samsung experienced an "Apple Shock" in its home ground. Within three days of iPhone sales in Korea, it captured 5% of the mobile phone market share. Koreans, early adopters of technology, fell in love with iPhones, and many criticized Samsung for being slow on innovation. A CEO of a large Korean conglomerate touted his purchase of an iPhone and encouraged his executives to use iPhones. Some even predicted that companies like Samsung would not last long.

But they didn't fully understand Samsung's DNA; the company gets stronger through competition and crisis. Thanks to the iPhone, Samsung was forced to move fast and innovate faster. In fact, the iPhone launch was credited for the promotions of many Samsung Telecom executives a couple of years later. How was Samsung so resilient?

Some time ago, I was invited to do a program for Samsung's Korean "dispatchers" on expat assignments in the USA. It was not long after Samsung's announcement of great earnings; however, the theme of the conference was like "Emergency Management." Despite Samsung's outstanding performance, there was a sense of urgency to make it better. Many Samsung employees agree that even during the year of their best performance, it is hard to get praises for their accomplishments. They rarely take time to celebrate their successes, although SEC gave a "special bonus" to all employees at the end of 2013 in celebration of the 20th Anniversary of New Management. While executives and employees are hugely compensated with special bonuses, there is a constant pressure for beating the last record.

KH saw "a sense of crisis" as one of the conditions for corporate longevity and emphasized constant transformation for survival. "Such transformation requires developing competencies to adapt to changes and eliminating non-essentials for businesses. If an organization gets too big, it will become bureaucratic, no matter how efficient an organization may be," noted KH Lee. In fact, some criticized Samsung Telecommunication's size for its recent "lackluster" performance.

According to a Chinese maxim, "There's no worry for the prepared." Samsung people do prepare for the future even more when things go well, because it's hard to stay at the top. Through vertical integration, Samsung has been able to minimize their risk. The loss from one group can be covered by the profit from other businesses. Yet Samsung wants all groups to be self-reliant and profitable, and each enterprise has to become more competitive as Samsung is committed to diversify sourcing outside of Samsung. Samsung will prepare for the future with what James Collins called "fanatic discipline" in his book *Good to Great*.

> *"What we call a crisis does not mean that we are facing tough times now. But it means to prepare for the big changes which we will have to face in four to five years. If we prepare for them well, we will be able to turn a crisis into a great opportunity."*
>
> — KH Lee

## CHAPTER 44

# Work Week—Mon., Tues., Wed., Thurs., Fri., Fri. and Fri.

When a corporate five-day workweek was introduced in Korea in 2002, banks adopted the system first. It was gradually extended to large corporations and small-to-mid-sized companies by 2011. Before then, Korean corporate employees worked half-days on Saturdays.

But even now, whether or not employees can take all weekends off vary depending on the company, function, team, boss, project, etc. So having weekends off is not always guaranteed. Despite Samsung's "Smart Work" effort, one Samsung employee described his workweek as Monday, Tuesday, Wednesday, Thursday, Friday, Friday, and Friday.

A workday can also be long, although it may not be intense the whole day. One Australian IT executive told me that he had jokingly suggested his customer engineer take a sleeping bag with him when he had to go on a business trip to support a Korean customer. Some Samsung labs already have foldable beds.

Given their long work hours, Koreans are reminded of a Chinese proverb: "Intelligent people can't win against hard-working people and hard-working people can't win against those who are having fun in the process." Korean business leaders understand that fun elements should be added to work for competitiveness, especially for the younger generation. With the ambition of becoming a great place to work for, Samsung is certainly aware of the work-life balance issue and the value of free time for innovation, such as Google's "20% time" initiative that allows employees to use up to 20% of their workweek to pursue special projects of their interest.

In recent years, Samsung has introduced more informal meetings venues (i.e. hiking a mountain, visiting a theme park or networking in a pub) that could be more conducive to generating creative ideas in a relaxing environment. It has also encouraged employees to take vacations. Some divisions of Samsung have also introduced telecommuting, "smart working" and flex time, allowing a four-hour workday after four days of working nine hours. But it's uncertain how many Samsung executives are willing to take a full week vacation, much less two weeks. Even during short vacations, most of them could be on call. One Samsung researcher talked about his boss who had not taken a vacation for eight years. A Korean Samsung executive commented, "How can some managers in the USA leave for vacation even when they have deadlines? How can they plan their vacation and purchase airline tickets several months in advance when they can't predict their workload? Those people seem to take their vacation more seriously than their job." It is not always easy to unlearn the lifetime habits of being hungry and hardworking.

Recently more Korean corporations started encouraging employees to use their vacation, however, Korean workers are expected to read the *nunchi* (an ability to size up a situation without verbal communication) of their boss and colleagues and to understand the context before they ask for time off. When a boss arrives at work before 6:00 AM, few employees would feel comfortable showing up at work as they please. Besides, many Koreans tend to prefer face-to-face communication because of high-context communication. Samsung also strongly emphasizes field management and speedy decisions. Thus, it will take a while for Samsung to allow telecommuting or flex time for all employees.

## CHAPTER 45

# Samsung Speed—Survival of the Fastest

" **I** n the past, big fish ate small fish. Now fast fish eat slow fish," said a Turkey's cabinet member in his presentation to American business leaders. If that's the case, Koreans can catch the most fish.

Koreans are addicted to speed. Samsung is not an exception. In fact, Samsung speed may exceed Korean speed. When Samsung built its fab in Korea, they built it in one-third of the time that would have taken other companies. No one involved in the project took holidays. The New Year or the Lunar New Year day was another workday. When imported semiconductor equipment was transported to the fab, they realized that the road from the highway to the fab was not paved. In a few hours, they completed the pavement and were able to transport the equipment.

It's not just in construction that Samsung showed the power of speed. Samsung spent only six months for a technology development project that had taken six years at Japanese companies. A foreign executive who joined Samsung was surprised that an approval for his R&D budget took less than a month. It would have taken at least six months at his previous U.S. employer. R&D team leaders frequently have decision-making power, not having to go up the chain of command.

Samsung also excelled in the speed of Supply Chain Management (SCM). A former Samsung executive credited speedy SCM for catching up with Apple. Through effective vertical integration process in house, Samsung has controlled the entire design and manufacturing process for smartphones, enabling Samsung to respond to the market demands faster.

Byung-Wan Kim, a former researcher at Samsung, speculated that developing the Galaxy S3 smartphone would take three to five months, whereas typical development time for a smart phone would be one year. That speedy execution was possible because KH doubled the R&D budget and recruited the best software engineers available. Some deplored that all of the good software engineers in Korean startups had been snatched away by Samsung in 2010, when KH returned to Samsung from his leave of absence. He requested of the R&D team, "Please make smartphones that are more powerful than any other phone in the marketplace." As usual, his order was a "mandate from Heaven" for Samsung executives and employees. Within three months, the Galaxy S3 was launched. One can easily imagine that researchers spent sleepless nights at work without going home.

There is definitely a downside to overemphasizing speed. A U.S. Samsung partner shared his observation: "The focus on speed and urgency compensates for lack of planning; very little emphasis on prioritization—everything must be done and it must be done immediately; however, if everything is urgent, nothing is really urgent." Nevertheless, a speedy process enables Samsung to accomplish its mission as "Digital-ε Company." "ε" stands for simplifying the decision-making process and speeding up development, purchasing, manufacturing and sales through the efficient use of information technology.

Some credit Samsung's speed to its meeting culture that maximizes effectiveness. Samsung's meeting guidelines are different from popular "Intel meeting basics," and emphasize meeting practices of simplicity and efficiency. With the belief that the key to a successful meeting is timing, Samsung adheres to three meeting principles:

- Set aside a day for no meetings.
- Limit the meeting time to one hour.
- Keep meeting minutes to one page.

Samsung also has a "Standing Meeting" based on a theory that a brain is most active when a person is standing with a deadline.

> "It's not the war between the strong and the weak, but the survival of the fastest… the faster eats the slower. If a war is not speedy, even if someone wins the war, the loss will be greater than the win. Speed is the essence of war."
>
> — *The Art of War,* Sun-Tzu

## CHAPTER 46

# Fight like a Pit Bull

Although Samsung's rise to the top in the global electronics market may appear sudden, Samsung has been a household name for a long time in Korea. It has been #1 in many categories. When Samsung enters into a new area, Samsung raises the bar and sets a new industry standard. "It's different when Samsung makes it" was one of Samsung slogans. So it's not surprising to hear that Samsung people can't live with any loss. Former Samsung Legal Counsel Yong-Chul Kim wrote in his book *Think Samsung* that KH had told his staff to "wipe out LG," when he found out that the sale of Samsung refrigerators in Korea was behind LG for one month, "...even if we have to give away Samsung air-conditioners and refrigerators free to all households with the profits from semiconductor and telecommunication units." Whether the statement is true or not is unknown, but it's good that didn't happen, based on BC's "catfish theory" that competition made them stronger.

Earlier in 2013, a blogger wondered how fund managers had missed seeing Apple's stock price going down. I wondered the same thing. Hindsight is better than foresight, but the signs of Apple's trouble at that time were visible to even a layperson like me. I was in Korea right after the $1 billion jury verdict against Samsung in the fall of 2012. Galaxy ads were everywhere. They set up booths at high traffic places, and there were long lines of people who wanted to try them. Samsung had a home court advantage and certainly won the sympathy of fellow citizens regarding the verdict.

In contrast, an Apple store in Seoul looked like a quiet library. Three months later, I went to Israel by way of Madrid, Spain. Samsung's Galaxy ads were much more visible than iPhones. It looked like that Samsung was ready to wipe out Apple smartphones from the market place. As one Samsung executive put it, the Samsung team "acted like a pit bull." Samsung looked ready to go all the way and would do whatever it takes to win. Even before the lawsuits, the fighting began. "Beating Apple is not just a goal. Our (Samsung's) life and death depends on it," revealed an internal memo to employees by Dale Sohn, which Apple presented in a trial. Sohn is a former president of Samsung Telecom America and now counsel to the President of Samsung Mobile. With that kind of determination, he was able to increase Samsung mobile's U.S. market share from 10% to 30% in two years.

"You die, I die" is an expression that Koreans use when they feel angered or wronged. A game is over when a fighter isn't afraid of dying.

So what's next? Samsung might have achieved beating Sony, but it is still too soon to declare a victory against Apple. Some people think that "Beat Intel" is Samsung's next goal. Samsung is second only to IBM in the number of patents earned in America for six consecutive years and Samsung received the most mobile patents in 2012. Samsung, looking to be Number One, may soon become Number One in all patents. But Samsung will need more than patents to fight battles against new fast followers.

## CHAPTER 47

# It's No Longer the Old Samsung

"**S**amsung is like a militaristic organization," says Sae-Jin Chang, a professor at the National University of Singapore and the author of *Sony vs. Samsung*. "The CEO decides which direction to move in, and there's no discussion—they carry out the order."

Samsung observers have cited speedy execution as one of Samsung's winning factors: Once the top makes a decision, employees just do it. While Intel and Amazon have the motto "Disagree and Commit," most Samsung people are not known for disagreeing with their leaders. A Korean organization's promotion system is often compared to an escalator, although exceptional talent can take an elevator to the top. Becoming a Vice President is like becoming a general in the military. So some leaders who have paid their dues to earn "stars" may exercise their authority and power in ways that don't inspire a new generation.

Samsung is still a hierarchical Korean organization, and there are some positive sides to running an organization like the military, especially when leaders know where they are going, what they are doing, and how to inspire their teams with a caring heart. Koreans emphasize the trait of "being humanistic" in interpersonal relations and they tend to work harder for bosses who show personal interest in them. A popular Samsung executive is known for remembering the personal details of his employees and their families. He tells his staff, "Your subordinates pay for your salary as you pay for mine. So I work for you." He regularly spends time with them in the evenings and on weekends to get to know them. He shows his concern about their well-being, sends texts on their birthdays and anniversaries, and goes hiking with his staff for teambuilding. In such a close-knit team environment, the mode of operation is not always command and control. A great leader like him seeks subordinates' input, listens to them and implements their suggestions. He challenges his staff with stretch assignments and gives them tools to succeed. Like a general who is loved and revered by his troops, he is admired and respected by his employees. Another Samsung VP tells his mid-level managers to "sell, not tell" in order to motivate younger generation workers.

The above examples may not represent the most typical management styles at Samsung. Recognizing the negative impact of authoritarian styles on employee engagement and creativity, Samsung started a group-wide campaign against "verbal violence" in 2013. Bosses who abuse their employees verbally will be reprimanded regardless of their rank and position. Examples of abusive language include: "How can you have a meal without doing anything productive? Does the food still taste good?" or "Your head is for thinking. It's not an accessory attached for looks." Koreans who are considered more emotional than other East Asians tend to use harsh words and hurtful remarks in hierarchical relationships, such as parent-child, teacher-student and boss-subordinate. Although the messages are not always taken literally and some may even be perceived as signs of caring, Samsung sees this as an area to improve to become a world-class company.

Appreciating such efforts and some changes in management styles, Samsung employees say, "It's no longer the old Samsung."

## CEO AS A COMMANDER

Several years ago, I went to Korea for a two-week business trip. On the third day after my arrival, an HR manager of a large Korean conglomerate called me to request a one-day program for his executive leadership team. The CEO was very keen on improving his team's executive presence and global presentation skills. Given the short notice, I had only one day to give him an option. I couldn't believe that all 15 leaders showed up, including one executive who had landed in Korea at 5:00 AM that morning from a business trip to the USA. The CEO wanted the program with all of his staff and got it. And everyone was fully engaged.

## CHAPTER 48

# Everyone Deserves an MBA

KH encouraged employees to invest in personal and professional development when he announced the 7:00 AM to 4:00 PM work hours in 1993. In an extremely competitive environment, Koreans are obsessed with upgrading their skills. It is common that corporate employees go to classes (language or other subject matters) before and after long work hours; many also study during commuting hours. Achievers like Samsung employees may try even harder than average corporate citizens in Korea. Many of them join internal study groups based on their topics of interest. They also get professional licenses and certificates to differentiate themselves from competition (often co-workers). Learning may continue even in the restrooms with magazines placed there. Samsung believes that ordinary people can become extraordinary talent through excellent choices they make on a daily basis. One day of discipline and hard work becomes a powerful force for an employee's positive transformation when it becomes a month, year and lifetime.

Given Samsung's global ambition, language skills are very important for those who want to be "global talent." Executives are given opportunities to take one-on-one language lessons with tutors. Some executives speak more than one foreign language. It is said that Samsung prefers people who score high on an English competency test because mastering a language requires discipline and hard work. Samsung wants talent with these traits. With Samsung's emphasis on China, Samsung provides Chinese language classes to employees and gives extra credit for candidates with Chinese language competency.

Even at executive levels, learning does not slow down because KH believes that knowledge is power for leaders. The executive offices I have visited looked like libraries. Like the founder who was an avid reader, Samsung executives voraciously read books. After they read books, they often summarize the key lessons and send them to their staff or pass the books around. SERI, Samsung's Think Tank, constantly publishes new books and reports on trends, economics, leadership and management that can be used as references for leaders. SERI was also used to hosting breakfast meetings (open to the general public) featuring thought leaders as speakers. There are endless opportunities for learning and development.

The critical theme for Samsung executive talent is effective self-management; they pay attention to health and self-development. They set aside time for exercise and learning.

---

### ASK AND YOU SHALL RECEIVE!

Samsung emphasizes that learners should study the heart of the matter. A few years ago, Samsung engineers were sent to a company in Belgium for a technology transfer. The team leader told them: "Learn the key principles. If they teach you one thing, ask two, three or five questions. If not, don't sleep. Don't think about coming back home until you master the key principles."

---

## CHAPTER 49

# Ethics and Integrity

S amsung's internal audit teams whose members include former prosecutors and law enforcement officers are famous for their thoroughness and toughness. While their functions have expanded to business process consulting in addition to traditional auditing, the name brings fear to Samsung executives, employees and partners because it has a reputation of "shooting down even a flying bird."

In February 2013, Samsung announced that it would incorporate the ethical business practices of its affiliates and executive-level managers into their performance evaluation. This decision was motivated by Samsung's desire to raise awareness of corporate ethics because its image was tainted by the recent fatal hydrofluoric acid gas leak and scandals from conspiracy and irregularities. The new assessment method will evaluate the performances of CEOs at Samsung affiliates by measuring their commitment to ethical business management and the outcome of relevant activities while they track any violations.

Ethical business practices are also emphasized in supplier management and procurement. In a very relationship-oriented culture like Korea, favoritism or nepotism easily takes root. Korea ranked the 46th in the 2013 International Corruption Index of 177 countries by Transparency International. The U.S. was 19th. Samsung is perceived as a relatively corruption-free company, compared to other Korean companies. A former advisor to Samsung wrote that Samsung purchasing department employees used to change suppliers often just to dissipate perceptions that certain suppliers were favored due to personal relationships. A company is run by people who have relationships with stakeholders, so Samsung sets specific rules:

- Do not accept money or flowers for congratulations and condolences for personal events such as weddings and funerals. (In Korea, they are frequently used for building business relationships and seeking favors. Cash is a common gift for such occasions.)

- Treat partners and suppliers to meals, if Samsung people happen to dine with them. If they pay, an individual meal cost should not exceed 20,000 won (less than $20) and it should not be frequent.
- Don't accept a gift certificate or gift. If it is delivered indirectly, try to return it. If it can't be returned, turn it into HR.

Breaking these rules has severe consequences. Anyone who is caught in unethical behaviors will face termination and the news will be distributed to all employees as a warning against any violation. Given Samsung's code of conduct, most Samsung employees are not likely to openly request meals or gifts from suppliers. In fact, some Samsung employees reportedly have told their suppliers, "Don't even think about treating me to lunch." Others even treat suppliers, but that is not uniformly practiced. However, Samsung is aware that the company can't ensure ethical behaviors of all employees, because it has over 400,000 employees. Vendors admit that some Samsung customers expect to be treated with meals or gifts, although not as frequently as they used to do. Several SEC managers were indicted in recent years for demanding entertainment or rebates from their vendors. The forms of entertainment included expensive meals, golf, yacht cruise, etc. Some even requested bribes disguised as personal loans.

But both parties must be aware that such things might be monitored, because any violations can be reported on Samsung's website. Vendors are also risking losing business with Samsung when they are caught in such unethical business practices.

## CHAPTER 50

# Etiquette Is Competitiveness

"Humanity and etiquette are part of competitiveness," said KH. Etiquette certainly is a ticket to success. In one international business trip, Samsung employees experienced the power of a warm heart and etiquette. Many years ago, several employees were sent to Marzotto, an Italian textile manufacturing company, for a technology transfer. Samsung was then a relatively unknown company, and the Marzotto employees weren't excited about teaching foreigners about their craft across cultural and language barriers. During breaks, Samsung employees noticed that Marzotto workers ate bread, candies or cookies they had brought from home for themselves. Unlike Koreans who shared even one small piece of chewing gum, the Italian workers didn't share their snacks with others. So Samsung's team leader asked his team to wear business suits to work in order to show respect to the Italian coworkers. They were also told to greet their Italian colleagues with a smile. Every day, the Samsung team prepared enough coins to buy coffee for Marzotto employees. Gradually the Samsung employees were able to build relationships over coffee with the Italian factory workers. As their comfort level grew, the Marzotto employees soon started sharing their knowledge.

Protocol is a word derived from the Greek *protokollan* meaning "first glue." The more protocol one keeps with another person, the deeper the bond they can build. And Samsung's coffee protocol became the glue to building relationships with Italians.

Good manners are emphasized at Samsung, even after work hours. In the past, Korean corporate drinking events were notorious for excessive drinking that lasted long past midnight. Some Korean males used alcohol for heart-to-heart, off-the-record communication without worrying about the hierarchy, but at Samsung self-discipline was very important. Even after heavy drinking the night before, Samsung men were known for showing up at work at 8:30 AM looking fresh and rested.

Samsung still wanted to lead a Korean cultural change regarding excessive drinking, and announced a company-wide anti-drinking campaign in 2012. It was not the first time that Samsung launched such a campaign. This time, Samsung was more serious. Samsung required employees to take anti-drinking training sessions and issued strict policies for workers. For employee gatherings after hours, they set up a rule called "119" (one place to drink, one alcoholic drink, and ending by 9:00 PM) for employees gathering after hours. Other companies soon followed suit. The significance of using 119 is that it also is the emergency number for fire and accidents in Korea. (In the U.S., it is 911.)

Interestingly, KH was known for not drinking much. Even in the company of drinkers, he was known to drink cider (tastes like Sprite or 7Up), although the premium brand of wines he had chosen for the events he hosted instantly became famous and received a huge following.

# VI

# Talent = Company

## CHAPTER 51

# Search the Globe for Three Geniuses

### Chairman of the Board = Chief Talent Officer

At Samsung Talent Development Institute, there is no President. The highest position is Executive Vice President. Who has been in charge of talent development at Samsung? It has been the Chairman KH Lee. Although he didn't hold the title, he was *de facto* Chief Talent Officer. He was that serious about talent.

Once he asked the Samsung leadership team to identify future business items. All the enterprise leaders worked hard to come up with their strategies to focus and grow their business in the next five to ten years. After listening to their presentation, KH smiled and commented, "We don't even know what will happen tomorrow. Then, how can we predict the business five to ten years from now? That's why talent matters. If we have the right talent, the talent will be able to effectively manage the change."

Long before many Western companies heralded the familiar mantra "People are our greatest assets," Samsung had put talent first. "Personnel affairs are everything," was Samsung's motto. "The only thing I'm greedy about is people," said KH. Thus, when JY, Vice Chairman of SEC and the heir apparent, was promoted to VP, his father KH gave him a painting that symbolized the importance of recruiting top talent.

Samsung's key talents are classified into three categories:

- S (Super): Demonstrate exceptional competencies, have global competitiveness, and deliver excellent results.
- A (Ace): Haven't reached the level of S, but possess great competencies and deliver strong results.

- H (High Potential): Not proven yet, but has a potential to become an S-class talent.

While these talents are nurtured and developed through special learning and mentoring programs, KH set the bar for recruiting talent even higher: "Find one genius who will take care of the livelihood of 100,000 people. My job is to find three geniuses like Bill Gates," he stated.

Why focus on hiring a genius? KH said:

> *"I have been thinking about what kind of business will 'feed us' (a Korean expression that will help them sustain survival and growth) five or ten years later, but I couldn't think of any brilliant ideas. Due to the fast pace of changes, it is extremely difficult to identify new businesses that will guarantee our future. Therefore, I came to a conclusion: our future livelihood will depend on a few creative people. A country's competitiveness will be determined by its creative talent."*

## CHAPTER 52

# Discover Tech and Design Talent

With a marching order from KH, hiring top talent has been a priority for Samsung executives. In 2002, Samsung tied 30% of executive compensation to recruiting and retaining top talent, so senior executives had to go out to the world, often offering candidates higher salaries than their own. Samsung was particularly interested in bringing in outstanding tech and design talent. About 10% of new hires are classified as S-class and a key S-Class engineering talent with a Master's degree or a Ph.D. can reportedly get the benefits and compensation given to the Vice President's level.

In the beginning of Samsung's global talent search, it recruited Korean brains working overseas. Samsung then hired talent across the globe: the USA, Japan, Russia, India and China. Especially after the financial crisis of 2008, many Japanese talents were available, and they contributed to Samsung's improvement in design and manufacturing.

In 2012, 25% of SEC global employees were in R&D and about 4,000 were dedicated to semiconductor research. *Chosun Biz* compared SEC's 365 Research Fellows to Jedi knights in *Star Wars* because of their power to face thousands of "imperial storm troopers." Their average age was 49.7, and almost half of them had Ph.D.'s.

In recruiting talent, Samsung looks for what KH calls maniacs. One definition of a maniac is a person who has an excessive enthusiasm or desire for something. KH himself has been called as a "film maniac" or a "sports maniac." At the same time, Samsung likes to grow maniacs as T-shaped leaders who demonstrate deep proficiency in a core function (the vertical part of the T) with wide range of capacities (the horizontal part of the T). Through the past experience of hiring purely technical talent, Samsung realized that they needed more balanced leaders with leadership skills and business perspectives. To develop such leaders, Samsung introduced a Techno MBA program for employees. Realizing that software talent will be a key factor for its future success, Samsung has also announced a plan to hire liberal arts graduates for software development positions. They will be trained for six months at the Samsung Convergence Software Academy. The program is partly due to a shortage of Korean software talent. Young Koreans have avoided majoring in computer science because the software development field has been considered to be a 4D profession (Dirty, Difficult, Dangerous and Dreamless) in Korea.

Blending technology with humanity was also emphasized at Apple. Steve Jobs ended his iPad2 launch presentation with the slide showing the intersection of Liberal Arts Street and Technology Street. "We believe that it is technology married with the humanities that yields us the result that makes our heart sing," said the legend.

U.S. higher education institutions have started responding to the call for the integration of technology and humanity. For the class entering in 2014, Stanford University has introduced a pilot program called CS (Computer Science) + X. X is a non-technology field of study, so Stanford undergraduate students will have opportunities to pursue joint degrees in computer science and music or English. Stanford plans to add other fields of humanities later for the joint degree programs with computer science. It will be interesting to see how Apple, Samsung and other technology companies utilize these talents for future invention and innovation.

## CHAPTER 53

# "SPEC" and Stories of New Hires

A couple of years ago, I had an opportunity to visit the Google campus in Mountain View, California. Drinking complimentary Google cappuccino, I was overwhelmed with the creative energy that filled every corner. But one Google training program ad posted on the wall perplexed me. The title was like "How to Motivate Unmotivated Employees." I asked my Google friend who gave me a campus tour: "Are there unmotivated employees even at Google?" He answered, "Yes, quite a few." His answer shocked me.

Are there any unmotivated employees at Samsung? Or is it possible to be unmotivated and still employed at Samsung? Samsung tends to attract talent with passion, discipline and a hard-work ethic in addition to a good SPEC. SPEC, an abbreviation of the English word specification, is popular "slang" among Korean job seekers. It means a combination of education history, GPA (grade point average), TOEIC (Test of English for International Communication) score and an English certificate or any professional license of a job seeker. Korean employees often evaluate job candidates' qualifications based on these criteria. Samsung HR executives have mentioned that SPEC is not as important as the unique STORY of a candidate; however, SPEC is not totally irrelevant. Still, graduates from top schools, including SKY (the initials of top three Korean universities—Seoul National University, Korea University and Yeonsei University and the acronym is also used to symbolize the difficulty of getting in to these schools, hard to reach like the sky), KAIST (Korea Advanced Institute of Science and Technology) and top foreign universities can have a very good chance of getting an interview.

However, Samsung has been working on hiring more graduates from regional colleges and high schools and trying to lower the barriers for them to join Samsung. Below are some criteria for new hires:

- Overseas education and training experience
- OPIC (Oral Proficiency Interview by Computer): Samsung has its licensing rights for Asia sales
- Graduation from a top university
- Internship or awards
- Volunteer work
- SSAT (Samsung Aptitude Test)
- Interview

With a growing emphasis on creativity, Korean companies, including Samsung, have been searching for talents with *kki* (loosely translated as "free spirit"). *Kki* is a Korean word that describes a unique talent for a certain area which the holder of the *kki* is eager to display and share with others. Good attitude also matters. Dr. Dae-Je Chin, former President of Samsung's Digital Media Business, liked to show a popular mathematical formula that equates the numbers of the alphabet with 1 through 26. While luck (L+U+C+K) adds up to 47,

- Knowledge = 96
- Hard work = 98
- Attitude = 100.

For new hires who don't have the right attitude, Samsung is willing to let them go. BC once asked a Samsung training academy leader, "How many people did you let go after the new hire orientation?" When he answered, "None," BC commented:

> *"You and I know that our recruitment process can't be perfect. If 5% to 6% of new hires leave the company in a year, we have wasted training money. So during the orientation, you need to teach them what Samsung is like and let them quit then rather than later. If someone wants to leave Samsung, the sooner, the better, for the employee and the company. If we keep the talent that doesn't fit, we may have to face a massive layoff later."*

## CHAPTER 54

# Samsung Talent "Military" Academy

Many U.S. corporations had an employee-training requirement of 40 hours per year. Even then, the training budget is often the first one to go during a recession. Samsung's average number of hours of training per employee was 112.5 hours in 2011. In comparison, a survey of American Society for Training and Development (ASTD) found that employees at 461 U.S. organizations had received an average of 31 hours of training in the same year. So an executive told me that everyone at Samsung could be qualified for a Ph.D. by the time he or she becomes a mid-level manager. No wonder that Samsung has a nickname of the Samsung Talent Military Academy where an ordinary professional is transformed into an extraordinary talent. Samsung strives to develop "creative, innovative and global talent." According to the website of Samsung Human Resources Development Institute, such talents can't be produced in a short period, but can be developed over a long period through systematic education. They undergo the programs and processes that require discipline and mental toughness. One female mid-level manager said, "When I look back at my achievement at Samsung, it feels like a dream. I had nothing special when I joined Samsung. I didn't believe in my capabilities, but my managers kept telling me that I could do it, so I didn't want to disappoint them." They are born again as Samsung men and women through discipline and hard work. They become possibility thinkers with a daring spirit to face any challenges.

For employees' continuous development, Samsung teaches a mindset for good learners. When employees go overseas for technology transfer training, they are told to empty their minds. They are encouraged to discard old thoughts and eliminate preconceived notions. Above all, they are told to be humble and not to think, "I'm too good to learn from others." They are reminded of the famous story of a wise monk who once lived in ancient temple in Japan.

## EMPTY YOUR CUP

One day a monk heard someone pounding his door. When he opened, a young student greeted him and said, "Since I have studied with great masters, now I am quite accomplished in Zen philosophy. But I have come to see if there's anything else that I need to learn and you can teach." The old master replied, "Come and have tea with me, and we will discuss your studies." The old monk carefully prepared tea, and began to pour the tea into the student's cup. When the cup was full, the old man continued pouring until the tea spilled over the side of the cup and onto the young man's lap. The visitor was startled and shouted, "You are a fool who does not even know when a cup is full." The old man calmly replied, "Just like this cup, your mind is so full of ideas that there is no room for any more. Come to me with an empty-cup mind, and then you will learn something."

## CHAPTER 55

# Invest in Building Glocal Experts

One of Samsung's most successful global talent development programs is the Global Regional Experts program. The "regional expert" contribution to Samsung's globalization was so strong that the CEO commented that Samsung had suffered from a $10 billion loss due to its late start.

Since the program was introduced in 1990, Samsung sent 4,400 employees (staff and assistant manager level) to 80 countries across the globe for total immersion. In 2012 alone, Samsung sent 350 employees overseas for the program. Each one cost $50,000-$80,000 per year. For the first seven years of the program, 60% of the selected employees went to advanced countries. After the year of 2000, more participants chose India, China, the Middle East and Africa as their host countries. The regions and the number of employees to be sent to each region are based on a 10-year market forecast of the target country population and growth potential for Samsung.

For the first six months, they focus on the mastery of language, and for the second six months, they travel around to learn local cultures and understand regional characteristics. Since Samsung values documentation for shared learning with colleagues, the employees must submit monthly reports. When they return to Korea, they receive continued support from the leadership team, and are placed in jobs that best fit their experiences. For example, many of the people who went to China through the program later became the key talent for Samsung's China operation. Their language competency impressed Chinese local hires and helped Samsung build *guanxi* (relationships) with stakeholders.

Given a high turnover rate of expatriates at multinational companies, Samsung sets a good talent management model for other global companies. Many expats often express frustration about their roles after returning to their home countries. Some are assigned to positions that don't utilize the insight they have gained from their overseas experience despite their employers' spending fortunes for the experience. In contrast, Samsung has been getting the maximum return on investment in their glocal (global + local) experts.

Another global talent program at Samsung is called the Global Strategist Program. Strategy consultants are hired from top international business schools such as Harvard, Wharton and INSEAD, and given an opportunity to work at Samsung Headquarters in Seoul. In the beginning, the turnover rate was high, but it has become more stable. With their bicultural understanding, they are building cultural bridges between Korea and other parts of the world. David Steele, the head of strategy and corporate communication for Samsung Electronics North America, is an alumnus of that program.

Also, through the Global Corporate Citizenship program, Samsung sends Korean executive and employee volunteers overseas for a short duration for community projects that help them expand their global mindset and humanity. The program has been so popular that applicants have to go through a very competitive selection process every year. And there is a side benefit: improving Samsung's corporate image around the world.

## CHAPTER 56

# Lee Daughters and the Rise of Samsung Women

*"Not utilizing women in the workforce is similar to riding a bicycle with one wheel."*

— KH Lee

In 1981 when I joined the Hyundai Group, women professionals were a novelty at Korean conglomerates known as *chaebols*. Hyundai was the first Korean *chaebol* that hired women college graduates for staff positions. While new male hires went to a field trip to Hyundai plants for a week as a part of new hire orientation, the women couldn't join the men because there was no dormitory facility for the women. Hyundai Construction had lots of projects in the Middle East then, so overseas assignments were required for career development. But I was told that women couldn't be sent to the region due to customers' religion. Twenty-five years later when Saudi Arabian oil company Aramco invited me to be a speaker at an executive summit in Dhahran, I experienced the famous "desert hospitality" from the host. Many executives were familiar with Korean companies, including Hyundai, thanks to numerous infrastructure projects they had undertaken in their country. The audience applauded with cheer when I told them that it had taken me a quarter of a century to fulfill my dream of visiting Saudi Arabia and that it had happened only via the USA.

Although Samsung and Hyundai competed with each other for the top spot in cutting edge business practices, Samsung didn't hire women professionals until 1992. That year, Samsung Group hired 250 women, mostly as secretaries and software developers. At least it was a large-scale addition to then male-dominated Korean conglomerates.

When Samsung does something, they want to do it right. Samsung created a task force to benchmark the hiring practices of IBM, GE, Deloitte, Corning and HP. In 1994, Samsung announced a plan to reform their recruitment policies, and KH ordered a drastic change in the utilization of Samsung women in the workforce, including equal pay for men and women. At other Korean companies, women were getting paid about 80% of their male counterparts, which some accepted as "reasonable" because women didn't have to serve in the military before joining the workforce. Samsung also placed women in positions such as purchasing and auditing, where women would face less discrimination because of their roles.

By 2003, about 30% of Samsung Group's new hires were women and women accounted for 40% of SEC's global workforce in 2011. According to CEO Score, a Korean company that analyzes management performance of Korean conglomerates, in 2013 Samsung Group had 50 females at a VP level and above, compared to 2,177 male executives. A former P&G marketing executive in charge of global marketing became the first female Executive Vice President of SEC in 2011. The youngest female Vice President was promoted from director within nine months of her last promotion. Such a promotion would normally take four years. She earned it for her performance in Argentina as an expatriate in charge of consumer electronics. Samsung recognizes and rewards hard-working women regardless of age and education.

A female manager who had joined Samsung with only a commercial high school diploma made the news when she was promoted to VP at SEC in 2013. Beside the deathbed of her father, she promised to him that she would take care of her younger brothers. To keep the promise, she joined Samsung after high school to support the family. Her first job was assisting semiconductor researchers with drawing drafts. She became curious about the subject and decided to study Japanese, because at that time most references were only in Japanese. As she mastered Japanese, researchers brought more books to her for translation and she became an accidental expert in the subject. She then enrolled in Samsung's in-house college. Her life story filled with sweat and tears became an inspiration for many aspiring young men and women.

SEC has a target to have 10% female executives by 2020, and is a leader in the number of executive women in Korea. Eighteen (44%) out of forty-one women executives who were promoted to VP level at the largest 20 Korean companies in 2013 were from SEC.

Did the rise of Samsung women have anything to do with KH's daughters? A successful man is often said to be proud of his daughter's achievement, while he wants his wife to stay home. His two daughters are top executives for Samsung subsidiaries. Like father, like daughter. Both are known as savvy entrepreneurs and leading *fashionistas*, and serve as role models for young Korean career women. KH's wife, an art major and well known art collector, is Director of Leeum Samsung Museum of Art with buildings designed by the internationally renowned architects Mario Botta, Jean Nouvel and Rem Koolhaas "to combine the past, present and future of art and culture."

## CHAPTER 57

# Leadership Wisdom from Asian Sages

According to KH, managing an enterprise is a performance art, and the CEO must be a comprehensive artist. He believed that CEOs must know technology and engineers must know about management. Thus, he emphasized literature and philosophy for leaders with a technical background. For leaders with a business and liberal arts background, he emphasized technical competency. It was clear that KH wanted well-rounded leaders.

Being rooted in Asian cultures, many leadership principles that Samsung leaders espouse are based on the teachings from Chinese classics. KH recommended Han Fei-Tzu (280-233 BC) as required reading for executives. Han Fei-Tzu teaches, "A third-class leader uses his own ability, a second-class leader uses another's power, and a first-class leader uses others' wisdom." Samsung executives frequently learn about the leadership principles of other Asian sages. For example, in 2012, Samsung Presidents attended a lecture on Lao-Tzu (604-531 BC), author of *Tao Te Ching*, by Professor Jin Seok Choi. Lao-Tzu said:

> *"A leader must lower himself like water and give credit to his subordinates. If he wants to take credit, they will leave him soon. If a leader frequently interferes with subordinates, they will protest. A leader's job is to create an atmosphere in which they want to do for themselves with enthusiasm and can fulfill their potential."*

According to Korean media, Professor Choi asked Samsung presidents: "Have you lived your life, doing what you wish to do?" and "Have you lived your life, doing what you like to do?" While his theme was leadership, the message was about the importance of understanding human nature in order to lead employees and connect with customers. He challenged them to create an environment in which employees will be able to do what they wish to do and what they like to do.

Confucius (551 BC-479 BC), another Chinese philosopher, was also a big influence on BC and KH. BC cited "*The Analects*" as the most influential book in his life. "I would be happy if my thoughts and actions are limited within the boundaries of the book's teaching," said BC. The leadership lessons of Confucius include:

- In meeting someone or seeing something, avoid preconceived notions.
- Don't say that things must be done only this way.
- Listen to other's perspectives with respect. Don't try to impose your ideas upon others.
- Don't think that you are the only one who can do a particular job.

SERI also promoted the leadership lessons from another Chinese philosopher Chuang-Tzu (369-286 BC). He taught leaders to practice the following for effective communication based on mutual trust and respect:

- Acknowledge differences between self and others.
- Tailor communication to the needs of others.
- Transform self through communication with others (with freedom from prejudices and pursuit of harmony).

Other Chinese classics on Samsung and other Korean executives' reading list include *The Art of War* and *Three Kingdoms*.

## CHAPTER 58

# Nurture Your Career
# like an Orchid

Large Korean corporations tend to utilize the executive hierarchy listed below:

- Chairman
- Vice Chairman
- President
- Executive Vice President
- Senior Vice President
- Vice President
- Director
- Senior Manager
- Manager
- Assistant Manager
- Staff

Samsung's performance evaluation system is considered relatively fair through vertical and horizontal evaluation. It takes about 18 years to progress from staff to director. About 0.6% of entry level staff rises to the rank of Vice President.

How do employees differentiate themselves from others to become executives at Samsung? Through continuous learning and development. They also work harder than anyone else. For example, the story of Gee-Sung Choi, Group Vice Chairman and the Chief of Office of Future Strategy, is legendary at Samsung. When he was sent to Germany to sell DRAM chips in Europe in 1985, he knew nothing about semiconductors. He was a business major at college, so technology was not his expertise. To overcome his weakness as a non-techie, he read and memorized a 1,000-page book about VLSI manufacturing process. He taught himself and asked experts until he understood the technology. Soon customers perceived him as an expert. To reach potential customers, he looked up the phone book, called any business that contained the word "computer" and asked them to buy Samsung chips. His first year sale of $1 million was record-breaking. Thirty years ago, Samsung was unknown in Europe.

To allow superstars to rise faster through the corporate ladder, Samsung reduced the time required for a promotion to the next level. It used to take 3-4 years to move up one rung of the ladder. Now a few superstars may reach the director level in 10 years. One can even skip a rung. For example, Samsung's Head of Mobile Design team who had designed Galaxy S3 was promoted from senior manager to vice president, skipping a level, at the age of 37. Of course, they are expected to deliver superior results consistently and may end up risking their career if they can't meet them afterwards.

Some say that a Samsung director has as much power and influence as the president of a small-to-medium size company in Korea, but it is a tough position because people at that level have to face "up or out" after several years. When someone is promoted to that level, an orchid is often sent to him or her. The message: the recipient needs to take good care of his/her career, like nurturing a plant that requires tender loving care. A taxi driver in Suwon, the home of Samsung's Digital City, shared a story of Samsung men crying in his cab on the day of their promotion: It is an emotional day for many of them. They are happy that their hard work with long hours has been recognized, but they are sad about the long and winding road ahead of them to get to the next level.

Aging can be a liability in a fast-changing society like Korea. It is not unusual in Korea conglomerates that middle level managers in their late 30s or early 40s think about involuntary retirement they have to face in less than 10 years. One mid-level manager in his 40s told me that younger employees had asked him, "Are you still working here?" In 2010, KH said, "Organizations must get younger or we will have to make it younger." Even if some interpreted it as his intention to smooth JY's succession by changing the old guard, Korean corporate employees, especially competitive Samsung men, might be under enormous stress to stay young and relevant.

It has been reported that some Korean males, not just females, go through plastic surgery to look younger. And it is considered essential for them to color their gray hair.

## CHAPTER 59

# Samsung Pipeline for Korean Leaders

KH emphasized five competencies for leaders: knowledge about technology, intuition about management, interest in computers, the first foreign language and the second foreign language. He also had a strong bias for action. Executives don't have time to sit in the office, because of KH's emphasis on field management.

As with every corporation, it can be risky to become an executive because it is a contract position, so some call it a temporary position. But many believe that it is worth the effort to become an executive at Samsung because most VPs and above don't have to worry about their career or livelihood after leaving Samsung. It is said that a VP at Samsung is set for life. A Senior VP won't have to worry about his and his children's finances. And an Executive VP will not have to worry about his, his children's and his grandchildren's finances. Senior VPs and executives above that level are given cars with full-time chauffeurs, secretaries, country club membership, etc.

After official retirement, executives are frequently given an advisor title with 70-80% of their annual salary and other benefits for two to three years. Some are invited to help with external relationships based on their vast networks.

Ex-Samsung officials are also very popular among headhunters. They are sought out as C-suite officers of Korean conglomerates or CEO candidates for small to medium-sized companies. For example, KT (Korea Telecom) has appointed Dr. Chang-Kyu Hwang, former President of Samsung Electronics, as its CEO. SK Group, SK Hynix, and Hyundai have also recruited former Samsung executives as their key leadership members.

Samsung executives are often compared to "strong and straight bricks" with reputations for being "clean" with company money. They are perceived as being good at managing company finances and being ethical with corporate funds. They are also recognized for strong strategic planning and execution skills based on global and local experiences. Samsung can be compared to GE and P&G as a key pipeline for developing Korean executives for other corporations. They are considered proven because KH has banned such behaviors as:

- Repeating the same mistake
- Lying
- Paying attention to trivial stuff
- Valuing only quantity and numbers
- Using ideas from low-level thinking
- Being complacently settled into their title and status
- Premeditating excuses for failures just in case
- Taking credit from subordinates or others
- Being preoccupied with office politics and
- Not developing people.

## CHAPTER 60

# The CEO Is a Global Headhunter

KH was known to call candidates directly to recruit the best talent. His global talent recruitment started with hiring Japanese advisors 40 years ago. During his father's tenure, he often went to Japan and invited top talent to his house for meals. He wanted to build personal relationships first so that they wouldn't think that they were betraying their country when they chose to join Samsung.

Reportedly, Samsung often paid top talent double or triple the salary of Samsung's Presidents and provided the advisors with translators, chauffeurs and maids. Once, Samsung had more than 100 technical advisors and 50 fab consultants who had retired from Japanese corporations. KH then actively searched for Korean talent working at global corporations like Intel, HP, IBM and Bell Labs. Former Samsung Digital Media President Dae-Je Chin and SEC President Chang-Kyu Hwang were among such top talents. The former worked at HP and IBM after graduating from Stanford and MIT. The latter received a Ph.D. from MIT and worked at Stanford University. Another example was Eric Kim, a Harvard MBA who was credited for building Samsung's brand image with its "DigitalAll" and "EveryOne Is Invited" slogans.

But the overseas recruits were not always welcomed by other Samsung executives. Kim, for example, recollected that he had never been accepted by homegrown Samsung executives and eventually returned to the USA as Chief Marketing Office for Intel. Interestingly other Korean conglomerates such as LG, SK and Doosan brought in non-Korean executives to Korea as C-suites executives as a part of their globalization efforts and they were also met with resistance. Later, some Korean-Americans were hired as consultants or contractors for a limited period. It reduced the resistance from "Samsung men" who had built their careers at Samsung and might have been threatened by outsiders.

From a global market perspective, Chinese corporations have adopted the strategy of hiring Chinese talent working overseas to globalize their operations and business practices. Japan did not send many students to foreign countries for advanced education and as a result, they had fewer opportunities to bring hybrid leadership to the Japanese corporate culture. Even now, India, China and Korea rank among top three countries of origin for foreign students on many U.S. campuses. Japan's insular approach may have hindered their recovery from recession, although Sony and Panasonic were ahead of Korean corporations in bringing non-native Board members.

In the 1990s, after the fall of the Soviet Union, KH ordered his staff to recruit Russian talent. At the time, a top engineering talent from the USA and Japan would cost $200,000 to $500,000 a year, but Russian talent cost a fraction of that. The contributions of Russian engineers to Samsung were significant. They introduced TRIZ, a methodology of systematic problem solving for innovation, which Samsung adopted in 2000 and Intel adopted later. In 2009, *BusinessWeek* reported that Russian brains helped Samsung develop the image-processing chips in its digital TVs and refine its frequency-filtering technology that significantly reduced noise on its handsets. Now Samsung is well on its way to being an employer without borders as it recruits the engineering student talent in China, Russia and India.

# VII

Sales, Marketing and PR

## CHAPTER 61

# Know Your Competition

*"If you know your enemies and know yourself, you will not be imperiled in a hundred battles; if you do not know your enemies but do know yourself, you will win one and lose one; if you do not know your enemies nor yourself, you will be imperiled in every single battle."*

— *The Art of War*, Sun-Tzu

*The Art of War* is strongly recommended by numerous Asian business leaders, including Japan's Softbank CEO Masayoshi Son and former SEC CEO Jong-Yong Yoon. It is an ancient classic, yet it provides modern business leaders timeless wisdom on competition and positioning to win a business war.

Since the New Management 1.0, Samsung has been working on knowing themselves and their enemies. Samsung semiconductor people study their competition such as Toshiba, TSMC, Micron and Intel to shape their strategies and positioning. For the smartphone space, Samsung must have understood Apple better than any other device maker. As its key supplier of parts, it would not have been so difficult for Samsung teams to predict Apple's product roadmaps with its orders. Samsung has also been closely watching the fast followers of China.

One of the questions BC used to ask before launching a product has also helped Samsung to win over the competition: Can people afford our products? Samsung has a wide price range of phones across the globe from Africa to Latin America. Samsung started producing affordable lower-end phones and added a premium brand later.

In contrast, Apple insisted on innovative higher-end products, until it was pressured to offer lower-end ones, as mobile phones became commodities. Samsung watches their competition and introduces products with enhanced features and mass-produces them when the markets are proven to be ready. Some argue that such a business model puts Samsung at risk because fast followers can quickly catch up to them with lower priced products that have equivalent or upgraded features.

However, once Samsung sets a goal against a competitor, they will do whatever it takes. KH told his people, "If you don't think that you can make better products than your competition, don't even start." Samsung needs to take heed of this before their product planning.

## CHAPTER 62

# Move Customers to Tears

S amsung suppliers often say that Samsung is a very tough customer. From Samsung's perspective, their demands may be just their right as a customer. Samsung has a high standard for customer intimacy and satisfaction. KH reportedly had said, "It's OK to smoke in front of your CEO, but it's not OK to smoke in front of a customer." In Korea, smoking in front of an elder or a senior without asking for permission is considered disrespectful. KH's statement summarizes his emphasis on respecting Samsung customers. For Samsung's sales training, internal sales "legends" share inspiring stories that show how Samsung goes above and beyond with exceptional service that can move customers to tears.

An ex-Samsung marketing executive shared a story in his book about a Samsung retail store salesman. A drunken middle-aged man was walking back and forth in front of a Samsung store. The salesman asked him if there was anything he could do to help. The man replied, "Today is my daughter's birthday. I was going to take a cake home for her, but I've left my wallet in a taxi and can't buy anything." The salesman presented the father with an MP3 player wrapped beautifully. To the customer's surprise, the salesman told the father to pay for it later. He was willing to pay out of his pocket if the man didn't show up. A few days later, the father returned to the store with his daughter. He not only paid for the MP3 player, but also bought her a computer. Later he made more purchases, including Samsung appliances. Due to the salesman's exceptional customer service and trust in his customer, the father became the biggest promoter for the salesman and Samsung products.

At Samsung, "customer service is not a noun, but a verb." KH said, "The reason why the word 'customers' is gaining more popularity over 'consumers' is because we need to adapt to each customer." He set an example for anticipating customers' needs. When Samsung opened the Samsung Medical Center, he checked in for three days to experience the facility as a patient. When he appointed his daughter to an executive position at The Shilla Hotel, it was reported that he had stayed there for a couple of months to experience it as a guest. He even ordered 300 books on hotel management and might have read them himself.

KH used a fable to teach employees how to satisfy the needs of customers:

> *"Once there was a little boy who lived in a village near the Yangtze River in China. The village leader was thirsty and dispatched the boy to bring water from the river. He wanted to give the leader the most tasteful water, so he kept going up the stream, searching for the perfect water. Several hours later he returned to the village with the water and wanted to present it to the leader. Alas, another boy had already delivered water to the village leader."*

The moral of the story: Don't waste time and effort without knowing the real needs of customers. This message is fundamentally different from the view of Steve Jobs who said, "People don't know what they want until you show them." KH emphasized meeting the needs of customers exceptionally well, while Jobs emphasized creating wants in customers. As for making customers happy, KH said, "If there's a dispute with your customer, do things that will please customers." So when Samsung chose to pursue lawsuits against Apple, one of its top five customers before the lawsuits, it must have been signaling a transition away from being an Apple supplier.

## CHAPTER 63

# D'Light Customers with Quality

S amsung D'light is Samsung's version of Apple's flagship store on Fifth Avenue in New York City. In the heart of Seoul's fashionable Gangnam district, the showroom is on the first floor of SEC's Korea headquarters. Technology lovers and potential customers can have a delightful Samsung experience with all the latest consumer electronics products by Samsung. The word D'light is a combination of "digital" and "light" that conveys their vision to be a "guiding light to the digital world."

As early as 1994, Samsung received Korean media attention with its New Declaration of Customer Rights. It promised to exchange a defective product within six months of purchase. This was a newsworthy offer in Korea, because Korean companies had very strict return policies then, if they had any at all. Samsung extended a product's warranty from one year to two years, and opened a Consumer Cultural Center that was committed to raising awareness for consumer rights and customer satisfaction. Samsung's new standard has set an example for Korean customer service, which is considered superior, even compared to Japanese service. Interestingly in Korea, the word "service" is often used for a complimentary offer and some companies find it a challenge to sell "service" products because some customers may expect those services to be free. For example, when a waitress at a Korean restaurant says, "This is service," to customers when she brings a dish, it means it is offered to them at no charge.

While Korean customers appreciated generous customer service when they had problems, Samsung knew that the best customer service was to manufacture the products that didn't need service afterwards. One Samsung VP was so passionate about testing and ensuring quality that he would throw a phone against the wall, smash it with his feet, drive over it, and throw it in the washing machine. Thanks to the relentless pursuit of excellence in quality, an SEC Vice Chairman once received a thank you letter from an IOC member from Peru.

> *"I dropped my Samsung phone on the way to the airport to welcome
> Prince Albert of Monaco. Then a four-wheel car that weighed two
> tons ran over it. I was worried about whether it was going to work.
> But then I heard my phone bell ring. Only the glass screen was broken
> and the quality of my call was excellent."*

That was certainly the ultimate way to delight customers.

## CHAPTER 64

# Product with a Soul

In 1996 KH emphasized that Samsung must make products with a soul and sell products with Samsung's philosophy and culture. In the mid-90s, Samsung was still an unknown company outside of Korea and the semiconductor industry. KH was aware of the importance of a country's image on national brands. Why are consumers willing to pay a premium for "Made in Italy" shoes and "Made in Switzerland" tools?

KH believed that if Samsung is going to be embraced by global consumers, Korean products must be perceived positively. If Korean products are going to be well-received by global consumers, they must appreciate Korean culture. So Samsung has been supporting Korean sports teams, cultural events and orchestras across the globe. Samsung and Korean companies are also benefiting from the Korean wave known as *Hallyu* thanks to the popularity of Korean entertainment since the late 1990s. For example, the success of a Korean television series *My Love from a Star* dramatically increased the overseas sales of Korean products that appeared in the series, including cosmetics, clothing and food. In the beginning, Korean dramas and K-pop were introduced to people in East Asia, but their popularity has since spread to the Middle East and Latin America.

About ten years ago, I was invited to critique presentations on U.S. market strategies by managers of Samsung's competing brand in Korea. Back then, Samsung consumer electronics had little brand recognition in the U.S., and Korea was an unknown country in the minds of American customers. Even the Korean auto company Hyundai was confused with the Japanese automaker Honda. So the managers didn't want to associate their company with Samsung or Korea. One manager even proudly said that their products were often perceived as European brands. Any customer's association of the Korean War and anti-government demonstrations was a liability rather than an asset to the company brand. I suggested that the managers collaborate with Samsung to build a strong Korea country brand for a win-win in the global marketplace as Toyota and Honda had done.

Fortunately, in 2009, the Korean government created the Presidential Council on Nation Branding to improve the "likability" and "credibility" of Korea, which would enhance the image of Korean products and services. Now with the mega-success of PSY's *Gangnam Style* viral hit song and the popularity of K-Pop and other Korean entertainment, Korea's global brand value has been on the rise. Korean cosmetics are already enjoying the "luxury" brand status in China and other Asian countries, so Samsung and other Korean companies can sell products with a Korean soul.

## CHAPTER 65

# Premium Brand Power

I n the Digital Age, products are differentiated by brand value and recognition more than ever. SEC has been implementing its global brand communication strategy since 1999. When Eric Kim, a Korean-American with a Harvard MBA, was hired as head of global marketing that year, Samsung's brand image was "fuzzy and inconsistent" despite having some cool products. It was partly because SEC engaged 55 ad agencies for their different markets and product lines. Sales channels were also uncoordinated, and some people worried that Samsung products were being marketed as second-class although they were easily first-class products.

Kim consolidated that work in a New York agency and ran a $400 million worldwide ad campaign. The results were dazzling. *Time* magazine reported on Kim's effort for Samsung's transformation in 2002: "Just a few years ago, Samsung was the brand you bought if you couldn't afford Sony or Toshiba. Suddenly it's the name that consumers seek out all over the world—especially young ones—for the most fun and stylish models of everything from cell phones to flat-panel TVs." *The Economist* also praised Kim's accomplishment during his five-year tenure at SEC: "Mr. Kim has unified the company's product development and advertising efforts into a cohesive brand strategy that gets the most out of the firm's impressive technology."

As one of the fastest growing brands in the world, in 2012 Samsung became a Top 10 Best Global Brand (# 9) on the Interbrand list, and climbed to #8 in 2013. In *BrandFinance*, Samsung ranked No. 2, only behind Google. According to an article in the UK's *Globe* and *Mail*, Samsung's investment in both marketing and R&D and its speed in launching new products led to the largest increase in brand value among the Top 10 in the rankings. Samsung's focus on design improvement was another key contributor to its brand's success.

With the increase in brand value, Samsung could afford to pursue a premium market strategy: In early 2013, SEC announced that they would identify some products under $200 to be eliminated. Samsung learned that high-end products brought higher profit margins even during the last recession. The Galaxy smartphones and Galaxy Note products contributed to a 20% increase in profit. Now that Samsung mobile products face stiff competition from Chinese companies, Samsung has to develop innovative products that can justify premiums through brand association.

# Topping Coca-Cola
# in Advertising

In 2012, SEC topped Coca-Cola in marketing expenses, spending $4.2 billion, or 5.4% of its sales revenue that year. Although the total expense was for all SEC product lines, not just phones, it spent four times more than Apple, according to a market research firm Asymco. Samsung spent almost $13 billion in marketing in 2013 and continued to fight against Apple and other fast followers for the top position in smartphone sales. With a huge marketing budget, Samsung has become a powerful advertiser in the U.S. For example, in 2012 Samsung increased its U.S. advertising spending by 58% to $881 million. For marketing phones in the USA, Samsung spent $401 million, compared to Apple's $333 million, according to ad research and consulting firm Kantar Media. Most of the expenses went to advertising Samsung's Galaxy in order to beat iPhone sales. *The Wall Street Journal* quoted executives of carriers, "Samsung also spends more on 'below the line' marketing than any other device maker. Those funds help pay for in-store advertising, promotions and training for carrier sales representatives that help close the sale." Samsung's investment in marketing and advertising has certainly resulted in a positive ROI (return on investment).

In Korea, Samsung's big advertising budget seems to influence the coverage of Samsung news. It is not so easy to find negative articles on Samsung in major Korean newspapers and other media. Some Korean media leaders may even refuse to run an article or advertisement that might damage Samsung's image. Samsung's "lobbying geniuses" have strong relationships with them. Also some editors of financially troubled newspapers in Korea reportedly have warned their staff not to write articles unfavorable to potential advertisers. It may be that money talks. It is well-known that corporate advertisers in other countries also put pressure on the media to run favorable stories as well.

Nevertheless, Samsung got negative publicity in Korea when it took a tough stand against a Korean newspaper, *The Electronic Times* (ETnews), which had reported an unfavorable article on Galaxy 5 before its release. In April 2014, SEC sued the paper and its reporter for damaging its product image. A few weeks earlier, ET ran two articles about a potential production delay of the new product due to lenses. While the paper insisted that the article was based on facts and interviews with SEC's key parts suppliers, SEC demanded a correction and an apology. When ET refused to do so, Samsung took it to court.

Some speculate that Samsung benefits from its strong family ties with the Korean media. *Joong-ang Daily*, a former Samsung company, is headed by KH's brother-in-law. *Chosun Daily*, with the largest circulation in Korea, and *Dong-A Daily*, another influential newspaper, are also related to Samsung families through marriages. Blood is thicker than water.

## CHAPTER 67

# Samsung Everywhere with Sports Marketing

S amsung is not the only company that sponsors sports events and endorses athletes. What is unique, though, is KH's foresight of trends and insight into sports. He predicted that golf would be one of Korea's exports items and that Korean players would be globally competitive. Before women's professional golf became popular in Korea, he had Samsung sponsor Se-Ri Park, a young female high school golfer, with a huge endorsement that helped her as she went on to win many LPGA tournaments. Samsung's marketing effect was astronomical, but what's more important was the development of "Se-Ri kids" in Korea who were inspired by her. Samsung was behind the dominance of Korean players in the LPGA: In 2013, five of the Top 10 LPGA golfers were Korean and 28 of the Top 100 players were Korean.

Many non-Koreans ask why Koreans are so good at golf. My answer is, "It's the 10,000 hour rule which was mentioned in the book *Outliers* by Malcolm Gladwell." Gladwell argued that one needs 10,000 hours of practice to acquire mastery of a skill. Many Korean golfers practice for endless hours. "Golf is the perfect sport for Koreans because it requires hard work," said a venture capitalist. KH must have noticed this Korean trait of discipline when he saw Korean golfers' competitive advantage.

Samsung is visible everywhere. Those who travel the world must feel Samsung's omnipresence from the moment they land at the airport. They can use complimentary airport luggage carts with a Samsung logo or recharge their smartphones in Samsung kiosks. On the way to the city center from the airport in most cities, people can see huge Samsung billboards on the most prominent places such as New York's Times Square and London's Piccadilly Circus. When they check in to a hotel, quite often Samsung TVs are waiting for them in their rooms. In October 2013, Samsung inked a $100M three-year deal with NBA (National Basketball Association) as the official handset, tablet and TV provider.

As a leader in sports marketing, Samsung is the most visible at all kinds of global and local sports events. Samsung owns its own professional baseball team (Samsung Lions), basketball team (Seoul Samsung Thunders), and soccer team (Suwon Samsung BlueWings). "All for Sports, Sports for All in Samsung," says a Samsung Sports website that is dedicated to sports marketing.

After being a local sponsor for the 1988 Seoul Olympic Games, it signed the TOP (The Olympics Partner) agreement with the IOC in 1997. Samsung's bid for the 2000 Sydney Summer Olympics cost nearly the same as its annual advertising budget; back then, it was considered to be a huge gamble. However, that worked for Samsung because as much as 80% of Samsung phone sales reportedly came from Olympics marketing. In 2007, Samsung extended its Olympic sponsorship through 2016. It ran "Team Samsung" for the 2014 Sochi Winter Olympics and Samsung will be a major partner in the 2016 summer event in Rio de Janeiro, Brazil.

Samsung's sport marketing has now expanded its scope to international competitions including the Asian Games, Paralympics and Youth Olympics. It also supports various International Athletic Federations in track, hockey and soccer. Samsung also sponsors sports teams in different countries, including England in which Samsung has sponsored teams since 2005. All these activities raise Samsung's brand image and contribute to increased sales across the globe.

## CHAPTER 68

# The Cheapest Way to Influence Opinion Leaders

Duringuring his first year in the faculty of Stanford University, Jim Collins, author of *Good to Great* and *Built to Last,* sought guidance from John Gardner, former U.S. Secretary of Health, Education and Welfare and the author of *Self-Renewal.* When Collins asked Dr. Gardner how to be a better teacher, he answered: "It occurs to me that you spend too much time trying to be interesting. Why don't you invest more time being interested?"

Samsung's founder knew how to be interested. When BC was scheduled to meet reporters, his staff had to provide detailed background information about them. With his intimate knowledge of them, BC was frequently able to turn journalists into friends. BC was known as a genius at lobbying. During his days, Hyundai people perceived that Samsung lobbying geniuses could accomplish anything (which meant they could win favors from the government and bureaucrats).

While KH avoided public appearances and rarely gave media interviews, he also recognized the value of lobbying. According to a former SEC executive, KH knew that leveraging lobbying expenses was the cheapest way to win friends and influence people and emphasized "moving, heart-warming services" for the people on the SEC's target lobbying list. The list in Korea was expansive, including key figures in the government, judicial system and media, and their "needs" would be taken care of, in exchange for the help they could provide in the future. At a minimum, flowers or wine gifts were sent to their homes on their anniversaries and children's birthdays.

After the lawsuit with Apple, Samsung increased its lobbying activities in the USA as it tried to influence the federal government on issues ranging from intellectual property infringement to telecommunications. *Bloomberg News* reported that

Samsung had boosted spending on lobbyists in the U.S. to $900,000 in 2012 from $150,000 in 2011. In 2013, Samsung paid the law firm Akin Gump nearly $1.3M for lobbying.

For public relations, Samsung knows how to use celebrities. Former U.S. President Bill Clinton spoke at the 2013 Consumer Electronics Show (CES) in Las Vegas as Samsung's keynote speaker. While Bill Clinton appeared as a civilian and promoted his cause as a philanthropist, it certainly was a big win for Samsung's publicity.

## CHAPTER 69

# Even a Lawsuit Can Be Good Publicity

Donald Trump once said, "There is no such thing as bad publicity." Despite the astronomical cost of lawsuits against Apple, Samsung didn't mind the world's attention. Apple's brand power was never challenged. The underdog image of a company that was fighting the No. 1 smartphone maker wasn't too bad for Samsung because it wasn't even among the top five smart phone makers in 2009.

The lawsuits created public interest about Samsung among global IT leaders and consumers. Even loyal iPhone fans were getting curious about Samsung Galaxy phones. Therefore, some Koreans commented that Samsung would not lose anything, regardless of the U.S. jury's decision. With the verdict, there was a concern that the lawsuit might reinforce the copycat image, but the attention and publicity were worth the risk for Samsung. However, with the market's lukewarm response for Galaxy S4 and S5, Samsung has to try even harder to stay as a market leader in innovation. In a notable move to change its design direction, Samsung Electronics' head of Mobile Design resigned in May 2014.

Giving a verdict of the Samsung-Apple lawsuits, jury members said that they wished that the two companies had settled themselves: ultimately, consumers pay the price. Thus, it was welcome news that the two companies agreed to end their patent litigation outside the U.S.

Has Samsung listened to Donald Trump for too long? Samsung's "The Next Big Thing" ad garnered a lot of attention in the beginning; however, the public has not been impressed with the continuous negative campaigns against Apple. They want to see outstanding, innovative products, rather than cynical advertising. If Samsung continues to negatively mention competitors in its ad campaigns, it will fall short of connecting with consumers. Samsung needs to remind itself of a Korean saying, "Even the positive comments are hard to take if they are repeated three times."

## CHAPTER 70

# Smart Social Media

With a smartphone business that produces more than 70% of SEC's annual profit, Samsung doesn't surprise us with its smart use of social media. Although Facebook CEO Mark Zuckerberg was reported to have chided JY Lee for not using Facebook during his visit to Korea in June 2013, Samsung is very active in the social media scene. Samsung Mobile is number one in the Twitter rankings among corporations. Samsung has an impressive web presence among IT companies. Samsung's websites are very informative and interesting. Above all, Samsung is interactive with its "Social Media Room" tab that engages its visitors. Samsung wants active participation from its fans, and fully utilizes bloggers. Samsung even recruits children bloggers with a separate website built for them. Samsung wants children to build strong associations with its brand starting from their formative years.

In Korea, Samsung hosts S Blog with dedicated bloggers. It holds Blogger Day Events for professional bloggers, and an event theme may be tailored to a specific product or service. In 2013, Samsung sponsored a Samsung Smart TV Blogger Day. Samsung also attracts global bloggers. For example, Samsung created "Everyone's Olympic Games" as an official wireless sponsor for the 2014 Winter Olympics Global Blogger Program.

As was the case in the 2012 London Olympics, Samsung used Samsung Network Services & Solutions (SNS) for Samsung's brand awareness and marketing. In London, Samsung invited young global bloggers to the Olympics to share the stories of athletes through SNS. In 2016, they also plan to operate "Team Samsung" that will support the Olympic athletes and wish the best for each country's players.

Some of Samsung's social media activities have generated more embarrassment than positive publicity. During the 2014 World Cup soccer, Samsung Mobile Arabia tweeted, "Best of Luck to Landon Donovan and the USA soccer team." Alas, Donovan didn't make the cut for the U.S. national soccer team in 2014; instead, he was a studio analyst for ESPN.

Samsung has been very aggressive in "buzz marketing," promoting its mobile devices through celebrities. According to a job description at Apple, a buzz marketer is "primarily responsible for constant and compelling exposure of products with high-profile users, especially those in film and television." At the 2014 Academy Awards, Samsung received mega publicity with the tweet of a selfie of Hollywood stars. The hostess Ellen DeGeneres had the picture taken on a Samsung Galaxy smartphone. However, shortly after that, another selfie got Samsung in trouble. David Ortiz, a Boston Red Sox designated hitter who has an endorsement deal with Samsung, tweeted his picture with President Obama and Samsung re-tweeted it. The White House expressed disapproval about Samsung's use of Obama's picture for a commercial purpose and implied it would open an investigation. A few weeks later, during his trip to Korea, President Obama told JY Lee that the photo was not a big deal. Yet, Samsung must control its excessive self-promotion, because overdoing it will be perceived as tasteless and result in a negative impact.

# VIII

## For Partners, Suppliers and Global Employees

## CHAPTER 71

# Know *Kap-Eul* (Customer-Supplier) Dynamics

*'It's not true that a customer is God. God is more forgiving."*

— Sales VP in Japan

In most Asian countries, suppliers are not equal to customers. Even if they use the word "partners" to describe their relationship, the customers have the upper hand. Koreans use a special term called *kap-eul kwan-gye* to describe the imbalanced relationship between a supplier and a customer: *Kap* represents a controlling customer and *eul* represents an obedient supplier. *Kap* is the stronger, and *eul* is the weaker. In Korea, *eul* is often expected to pay for meals and entertainment with *kap*, including golf outings. Kap's subtle requests or overt pressures, despite being unethical or illegal, can include jobs for children and large gifts for family members.

Although most suppliers across the globe agree that the customers rule, Samsung is considered as "Super *kap*" because of its domineering power. Samsung partners often feel that they are at the mercy of Samsung. One former Samsung Korean supplier said in a press interview that he used to park his car in a Samsung parking lot far away from his meeting place to demonstrate his lowliness and show utmost respect to his Samsung customers. Another executive of a top international management consulting firm said, "Samsung considers any vendor as a subordinate or servant, not a partner. Even bankers and strategy consultants who work with Samsung are treated very harshly because Samsung wants to show them that they have the upper hand." His advice for suppliers, "Don't take Samsung's attitude personally. Every supplier is in the same boat."

Samsung wants a speedy response and doesn't want to hear "no" to their requests. It's hard for vendors to plan holidays and vacations, when their customers rarely take time off. At one company, a Samsung account manager position was considered to be a set-up for failure because very few lasted for more than one year. Many suppliers have a lot of Samsung survival stories to tell. They find aggressive deadlines and lack of information sharing (with vendors) as big challenges in working with Samsung.

Nevertheless, Samsung is still a coveted customer for many vendors because of its volume and prestige. And most of them agree that Samsung is not the only difficult customer in the world. Even some Samsung suppliers admit that customers in general are tough on their suppliers and others confess that they themselves are hard on their vendors. And there are reasonable customers at Samsung too.

It is still critical to choose culture-savvy employees for the positions who interact with Samsung and other Korean companies. In many Asian countries, it is generally accepted that the customer is king or even God. Despite these hierarchical relationships between a customer and a supplier, there are people who enjoy the Samsung Way and appreciate the Korean way of doing business. They are more likely to accept that they don't get to choose their customers. So they try to make the most of the engagement.

## CHAPTER 72

# Build Relationships, but Be Aware

"Network is net worth." Relationships are important in doing business with any culture. Especially, if you are a supplier, it is important to invest in building relationships with customers. You need to learn at least three personal, non-business related facts about them. Samsung sales people are known to remember the birthdays, wedding anniversaries, golf handicaps, family details and even eyesight prescriptions of their key customers and partners.

A successful U.S. supplier's sales executive befriended Samsung managers and earned their trust. When they visited the United States, he treated them at Korean restaurants. When engineers came for an extended stay, he took them to Korean grocery stores. Since his company had a guideline for entertainment, he used his own funds to get to know them. He even learned basic Korean phrases and attended "Working with Koreans" workshops. Many Koreans appreciated his effort to better understand customers. He didn't do these to get business from them. He had a genuine interest in Korean culture and people. When Samsung wanted to lower the price, he would say, "Samsung, don't you want us to stay in business? What would happen to Samsung if we cease to exist? It won't be good for you either." Although Samsung didn't always pay the price he wanted, he made his customers laugh and sustained their goodwill with positive relationships.

Relationships are also critical to obtaining information and feedback. Samsung treats almost everything as confidential, so suppliers often have a hard time getting access to necessary information which Western customers are willing to share. Suppliers may only be able to get pieces of information through personal relationships and informal meetings in order to connect the dots. It tends to take longer to earn trust from Samsung than other Korean companies, but relationships still matter in the end. One Samsung executive said, "These days most vendors are very competitive. They have similar offerings in price, quality, service, etc. Then I prefer to work with 'pleasant' vendors who have shown genuine interest in us, stayed in touch with us, and made an effort to build relationships with us."

Harvard Law School's *Program on Negotiation Special Report* cited Professor Cheryl Rivers of Queensland University of Technology in Brisbane for cultural differences in negotiations. She concluded that Asians are more likely than Americans and Canadians to view as ethically appropriate the cultivating of a relationship with a negotiating counterpart by using expensive gifts, entertainment or personal favors. Samsung is an exception to these tendencies.

If you are doing business with Koreans as customers, don't be naïve. If you are in procurement, don't be tempted by "relationship-building" events or gifts. Naturally hospitable Koreans know how to entertain their customers. Don't do anything that you are going to be embarrassed about if others find out. Nearly everyone has a camera phone, so you can't control what will be posted on the Internet the next day. Also, "special favors" can be used against the companies or recipients later.

---

## THERE IS NO SECRET

During the Han dynasty in China, there was a period of political chaos. The government was filled with corrupt bureaucrats. However, a governor of one province was a man of integrity. One night, a businessman came and presented him with a pile of gold as a bribe. The visitor said, "Please accept this. Nobody will know about this." The governor scolded him and said, "The Heaven knows, the Earth knows, I know, and you know. How could you say that no one knows?"

## CHAPTER 73

# Do Due Diligence for Negotiation

In negotiation, when your partners know more about you than you know about them, you are at a disadvantage. Considering that Samsung is a master of business intelligence, it would be wise to stay on guard. Below are a few tips for negotiating with Samsung:

- Do research on the background of your counterparts, including their education, work experience, reputation, personality, etc.
- Hire your own translator and brief him/her in advance.
- Don't be a lone ranger. If your travel budget allows, go to a negotiation meeting as a team.
- Engage a cross-cultural consultant or an advisor who understands global business practices and has done business with Korea.
- Know when to retreat. If things are at a deadlock, take a break and revisit later. Time your persistence well.
- Saying "no" gracefully is better than saying "yes" grudgingly.
- Understand that some Koreans' lack of eye contact is not necessarily a sign of disrespect.
- Have a sense of humor.
- Stay calm when Koreans get emotional at times.
- Leave some room for items or services to be given away free during a contract period for goodwill.

Even in dealing with tough negotiators, you don't have to give in to customer demands all the time. I have heard about Samsung negotiators who asked for an additional 15-20% discount even when they were given the best price among all customers. If your products or services have comparable advantages over competitions, you may be able to stand your ground. If you know when to be firm, you will gain more respect. Vendors say, "The only time Samsung doesn't use a hard bargain is when our products are superior or they are running out of time." But even when you know that Samsung's options are limited, it is important to maintain a collaborative spirit. If they feel overcharged in one way or another, Samsung will remember it in the next bidding cycle.

At the same time, don't take their words at face value, even if they talk as if it were a done deal. A former executive of a top U.S. consulting company said, "Samsung customers frequently backed out when I asked for a written engagement agreement after they said that they were ready and asked me to assign consultants for the project." Patience is a virtue here. Even if Samsung is known for speedy decision-making, some projects can take longer than expected, especially if one requires a large capital investment that will need a blessing from the top or public relations management in Korea. The good news is that once a decision is made and an agreement is reached, execution is relatively fast at Samsung.

## CHAPTER 74

# Soften Your Energy
# and Save Face

Everyone emanates energy (*ki* or *chi*) from his inner spirit and sends invisible waves to others. Many Asians are reluctant to do business with people whose *ki* seems to be in conflict with theirs. They can feel it even without saying a word, because people send and receive energy. A former SEC President Chang-Kyu Hwang described a negotiation with the late Steve Jobs as a "*ki* fight." Their encounter must have been intense for both, smart and strong, who wanted to tap their energy to their advantage and dominate over each other.

According to the Chinese yin/yang principle, the universe/society/individual should have both yin (feminine, water) and yang (masculine, mountain) energy for balance and harmony. Yang is hard, aggressive, and penetrating. Yin is soft, gentle, and embracing. Yang (Sun) energy is powerful when it is balanced with yin (Moon) energy. Unless it is properly managed, one's excess yang energy leads to confrontation and burnout. Anyone who has too much yang energy would benefit from softening it around Korean customers if he/she wants to build rapport with them. If you have overly intense eyes, for instance, soften your gaze by imagining a dimmer switch to lower the intensity of your gaze. Lao-Tzu teaches this:

> *"Nothing in the world is as soft and yielding as water.*
> *Yet nothing can better overcome the hard and strong.*
> *For they can neither control it nor do away with it.*
> *The soft overcomes the hard. The yielding overcomes the strong."*

Show respect while avoiding conflict and confrontation. Building relationships and saving face are the keys to effectively engage and dialogue with your Korean counterparts. Most Koreans don't perceive being direct as being honest. Rather, straight talkers may be considered to be lacking emotional or social intelligence. In fact, "being straightforward" has a negative connotation in Korea. It doesn't mean that you have to agree with everything you hear. But you would be wise to avoid saying bluntly, "I don't agree with you." Instead, you may try "I have a slightly different idea," or "I might add something to your idea." Consider the impact of your communication on the feelings of the receivers and protect their social esteem in a group. It pays to be an easy person to be with.

"*Kibun*" (one's emotional status) is very important to Koreans. The same proposal may be accepted or rejected depending on one's *kibun*. So make sure that your words or deeds will not negatively affect one's *kibun*. And it's worth paying attention to non-verbal communication because it can send unintended messages. A U.S. executive of a Samsung's partner company showed up wearing jeans in a meeting with Samsung executives. To avoid the sunlight in that office, he was also wearing sunglasses. Later Samsung executives shared their negative perceptions of him with the company's Korean representative. Since then, the company required a Korean cultural briefing of anyone who did business with Korea.

## CHAPTER 75

# Don't Try to Educate Customers

A global study of 6,000 sales reps across 100 companies by Conference Executive Board (CEB) found that "challengers" are 4.5 times more likely to be high performers in complex sales environments by building constructive tension. "The best sales people don't just build relationships. They challenge them," states the CEB website: They teach customers, tailor their sales message to customers, and take control of the sale. They focus on sales conversation on insights, a unique perspective on customer's business, rather than on features and benefits. In fact, when I worked at a large multinational consulting company, we consultants felt free to share what we knew with clients through open discussions and clients valued our insight. Korean customers also appreciate new knowledge and insight from consultants and suppliers, but it should be delivered in the right manner. Some westerners who "know it all" and are eager to educate their Korean customers may end up offending them, even if they have good intentions. Overly straightforward communication is not appreciated.

Samsung customers tend to be proud, so it is especially important to be humble and respectful in dealing with them. When a vendor disagrees with them, they may say "Do as I say" rather than try to find solutions together. Don't quickly brush them off as unreasonable or inflexible. To get buy-in from customers, you need to:

- Build rapport with them by engaging in a small talk.
- Ask the right questions.
- Listen to their perspectives.
- Try to see from their perspective and see whether their views have any merits.

- Position your solution to their advantage.
- Be humble. Don't think that you have all the answers before you fully understand their problems.
- Repeat politely without reminding customers of earlier discussions or agreements, even when they want to revisit the items that had been settled. Don't say, "I have already mentioned that several times."
- Pay attention to "face-saving" behaviors. Avoid putting your Korean counterparts in embarrassing situations.
- Use a respectful tone and body language. (For example, crossing your legs in front of senior leaders or customers would be considered inappropriate. Also calling them out with the index finger is not acceptable).

---

## THE POWER OF AN APOLOGY

A sincere apology can be the best way to build trust and earn respect. A Samsung supplier in Israel made a mistake on a Samsung project. Its executive flew to Korea immediately and apologized to a Samsung VP and told him how they were going to fix it. The Korean VP told him, "Now we trust you. We can work together again." In Korea, an apology can be used to show your empathy for their inconvenience even when it is not your mistake.

## CHAPTER 76

# The Art of Cross-Cultural Communication

Most global teams cite communication barriers as the biggest challenge for working internationally. One of former SEC's top executives said, "It takes three times longer to read an English document than a Korean document." Another executive said, "I still understand only about 70–80% of business conversations conducted in English." An employee of a U.S. Samsung supplier wrote, "In a one-on-one discussion with a Korean partner, we both agreed that we only understood about 50% of what the other one was saying. We agreed to ask questions until we understood 100%."

In addition to the language barrier, cultural differences also create a gap between intentions and perceptions. Korean perceptions of American communication styles include:

- Talk too much (Discuss a lot).
- Speak their mind (Everyone has an opinion).
- 'No' is very clear.
- Don't understand the context.
- Overly confident, as shown in expressions such as "Can do!" and "No problem!"
- Exaggerating: Overuse of "Terrific!" "Fantastic!" "Absolutely!"
- Impersonal (e-mail over face-to-face communication).
- Animated.
- State the obvious (Low context).
- Never apologize for mistakes.

Given these perceptions, when you communicate with Koreans:

- Check your assumptions.
- Speak clearly and slowly.
- Avoid slang, jargon, and idioms.
- Be aware of hierarchy ("peer culture"): Understand your place in the pecking order.
- Demonstrate personal warmth and sincerity.
- Read *kibun* (feelings).
- Save face and preserve harmony.
- Have one-on-one meetings for additional input.
- Use informal occasions for building relationships.
- Don't take it personally.

As for a preferred medium of communication, Yong-In Shin, the author of *Samsung vs. Intel* who worked at both companies, summarized the cultural differences between two companies: Samsung mobile vs. Intel email. Koreans' addiction to speed is reflected in their communication. With their common use of the expression *ppali-ppali* (hurry, hurry), Koreans want instant feedback and response. *Katalk* (the abbreviation of *Kakao Talk*) is used commonly for instant text messaging, and calls are expected to be answered promptly. Most Koreans don't like voice mails. While Koreans want instant response or feedback from partners, Korean counterparts are known for no or slow feedback, especially in emails. So if you need a quick response from them, it will be better for you to pick up the phone.

## CHAPTER 77

# Read *Nunchi* and Expect *Kimchi*

Korean word *nunchi* means an ability to size up a situation often without verbal communication. With a relatively homogeneous population, Koreans take pride in reading each other's minds with few words. *Nunchi* is an important social skill for Koreans in various contexts. Wives use *nunchi* to read their husbands' true intentions, and subordinates are expected to use *nunchi* to understand their bosses' expectations. *Nunchi* is also used for communicating among peers. A mastery of *nunchi* is particularly appreciated when direct communication would cause discomfort for a speaker and/or a receiver. It is an art that Koreans develop from childhood.

A senior executive of a major conglomerate said that *nunchi* is more important than work itself, and many Koreans agree with the statement. A person who doesn't possess *nunchi* lacks very important interpersonal effectiveness at a Korean workplace. An American manager hired by a Samsung U.S. subsidiary could not read the *nunchi* of his new boss who had just arrived from Korea. The manager could sense that the boss wasn't happy with him because he kept avoiding him. Finally the American scheduled a meeting and asked him: "What do you want me to do?" The Korean boss answered, "You should have known that already."

Dr. George Simons, a brilliant colleague of mine and author of many diversity books and games, compared the feedback styles of Americans vs. Koreans by using the visual images of food: a hamburger vs. a collection of Korean side dishes, including *kimchi*. The interpretations vary depending on one's perception, but it's easy to recognize the differences. The buns and a beef patty represent soft, hard and soft feedback. For example, an American boss may say to his subordinate, "Thanks for completing the report on time. But I've found key data missing. I will appreciate it if you can redo that part. Keep up the good work." In contrast, a Korean boss might take the spicy *kimchi* approach and only point out the missing data. Feedback may also come piece by piece, which makes it difficult for foreigners to grasp.

Some suppliers are often frustrated with Korean customers' unclear requests: Instead of being specific on their wants, Some Korean customers say, "Just do what you think is necessary." Because of the implicit, high context nature of *nunchi* reading, it can cause miscommunication unless you have an expert *nunchi* translator.

While Koreans frequently use indirect communication, there are occasions on which they speak very bluntly. When they give negative feedback to lower level employees or vendors, they come across very rude. Many Westerners are discouraged when Koreans don't express gratitude or give positive feedback for their hard work, but you should not take it personally.

A former U.S. Samsung partner wrote: "I have experienced certain conflicts with Korean middle managers. They make unduly negative statements about my company in meetings where their Korean superiors are present, and I am told later that they do this because they must appear to be aggressive and dominant (toward vendors) to their bosses. It is like they are two different people, when the big bosses are around, and when they are not."

## CHAPTER 78

# Share Only What You Are Willing to Lose

Some suppliers are concerned about Samsung as a competitor. They worry that once they share their technology, Samsung may develop it internally or give the work to another Samsung entity or a Korean vendor. Since Samsung tends to do a lot of things in house, it is conceivable. It would be prudent of any suppliers to carefully guard their IP or they may share only if they are willing to lose it.

However, Samsung can't do everything alone. They need to create external competition with partners and suppliers so that the employees won't stay complacent. Samsung also wants to maintain the equilibrium in a supply chain. They don't want a vendor to dominate a market because they want bargaining power. It's smart to have more than one supplier anyway, just in case of a supply shortage due to unexpected disasters or market changes.

In 2013 Samsung announced a plan to reduce the percentage of purchases from other Samsung entities, giving more opportunities to non-Samsung vendors. In fact, Samsung surprised industry watchers with its announcement to buy DRAM Chips from its competition SK Hynix. An SEC senior leader was reported to have said, "If only when I am well, I will be able to share with my brothers," when the leaders of other Samsung divisions asked him to buy parts from them.

The suppliers who are uneasy about losing IP will have to do due diligence for any potential threat of losing their IP. It will be wise to ask those who have done business with Samsung about their experiences. Also, a culture-savvy negotiation team will be helpful to get paid for a licensing agreement.

At the same time, suppliers should prevent unintended, complimentary technology transfers through human communication. Free knowledge transfer can happen unintentionally at bars or restaurants. Some engineers may brag about their newest projects after a couple of drinks, while competitors at tables nearby are listening for intelligence. So it would be prudent to remind employees of security guidelines and reinforce them as Samsung does with their employees.

## CHAPTER 79

# Connect with the Human Side of Koreans

Western suppliers who do business with Korea often have these perceptions about Koreans:

- Abrupt (rude)
- No facial expression
- Lack of eye contact
- Harsh and unclear
- Formal
- Lacking commitment
- Vague and hesitant
- Lack of documentation
- Reserved
- Save face
- Blunt and Direct
- Polite
- Respect rank
- Yes doesn't mean yes

Of course, perceptions differ depending on their customer's corporate culture, generation and functions.

Samsung people, despite KH's emphasis on humanity, are perceived as lacking warmth compared to the employees of other Korean companies. Even as a facilitator or instructor, I notice cultural differences among various corporations. Samsung people tend to be more formal. Many act so professional to the point of being unapproachable. They tend not to engage in small talk or joke around during classes, although there are exceptions. It seems that the higher the title, the better sense of humor an executive tends to show. Below the surface, Samsung men still share Koreans' warm heart and many do have a great sense of humor. At a wireless conference, I met an American mid-level manager who used to have a Samsung account at a U.S. telecommunication company. He missed working with Koreans, because they were so much fun. Winning a customer's heart will be the key to increase his desire to help you and your business.

Like many Israelis who are compared to a Sabra cactus because they talk and act tough but have a warm heart, serious-looking and tough talking Samsung men can be warm and personable. Due to company rules and procedures, they may not want to be too close to suppliers. And due to cultural and language barriers, they may not know how to express their human side and make Westerners feel comfortable.

One American Samsung employee told me about his former boss who was a Korean dispatcher. He was difficult to work for. They did not have a close relationship during his assignment. But then the American ran into his old boss at a meeting in Korea. The boss introduced him to everyone: "This is my buddy from the States." The Korean manager also extended help for the American's project. The American couldn't believe the generosity he was shown. Most Koreans often use the term *jeong* (emotional bond) built not only through positive experience, but through negative ones as well.

So don't despair if your Korean counterparts are difficult to get along. Be the nicest person you can be and try to connect to the human side. Samsung people also understand global humanity.

> *"To be part of the Asian dynamism, Westerners do not need to become Asians in culture, in values or in habits, but it is necessary for Westerners to understand Asians, to feel at ease with Asians and to make Asians feel at ease with them."*
>
> — Kuan-Yew Lee,
> Former Prime Minister of Singapore

# IX

# Feedforward* to Samsung: Suggestions for the Future

*Feedforward is a term created by management guru Marshall Goldsmith. While feedback is often critical of the past and makes the recipient defensive, feedforward suggests solutions for the future and gives the recipient a positive framework for change.

> *"We can change the future. But we can't change the past. Negative feedback tends to produce defensiveness on the part of the receiver and discomfort on the part of the sender. Feedforward helps people focus on a positive future, not a failed past. It focuses on solutions—not problems."*
>
> —Marshall Goldsmith

## CHAPTER 80

# Innovate Smart with a Soul

*"There are three ways to win: make products cheaper than everyone else, produce them faster than the competition, and create products that have not been made by others."*

— BC Lee

"In the past, we were guided by the lighthouse—[many] leading companies in the advanced countries, but now we are at a position in which we have to discover our own paths in uncharted territory," said KH in a speech to his employees in 2013. Now Samsung needs to create its own course in an endless sea. There are many reasons why Samsung must be paranoid. Korean companies benefitted from the high Japanese yen for the last several years. However, with the yen's devaluation, Japanese products may appeal more to global customers, and Korean manufactures can no longer enjoy a comparative advantage over Japanese in prices.

Even if Samsung has a competitive advantage with premium design and quality, corporate rivals in China, India and other parts of the world are chasing Samsung. Chinese manufacturer Huawei already has over 70,000 R&D employees. Xiaomi, a Chinese smartphone manufacturer, has become a serious competitor. In early 2013, after attending the Boao Forum in China, an Asian version of the World Economic Forum in Davos, JY reported that China research institutes had many task forces studying Samsung. From a talent management perspective, Samsung (and other Korean companies) may face a potential exodus of experienced professionals in a few years. During the Japanese recession, many Japanese executives and engineers left corporate Japan and chose the Samsung ticket. Like those Japanese who facilitated Samsung's dramatic change and growth, Korean design and tech talent will be open to consulting Chinese and Indian companies for opportunities outside of Korea. Korean baby boomers (who were born between 1958 and 1963) are already forced to retire, so such options will be more appealing to those executives who have limited career opportunities in Korea due to their age. There is no guarantee that ex-Samsung executives or employees will not advise new fast followers like Huawei, ZTE, Lenovo and Xiaomi. According to a *Korea Economic Daily* article on talent migration, Chinese smartphone companies have already started hiring Korean manufacturing or technology leaders from Samsung and LG.

Samsung was ranked No. 17 among the "World's 50 Most Innovative Companies" by *Fast Company* (March 2013). Given that Apple was ranked 13th, Samsung scored well, but the reason for its selection was not flattering: "for elevating imitation to an art form." Apple is considered as a company with a soul, but Samsung is not. Samsung still has some work to do in order to build emotional connections with customers.

Samsung's challenge in transforming its image is captured in management guru Marshall Goldsmith's book title, *What Got You Here Is Not Going to Get You There*. Samsung will have to think faster and act smarter to get there. With his 3D thinking and keen perception of the times, KH might have been envisioning breakthrough products no one has made. Since the beginning of 2013 until his hospitalization in May 2014, he spent more time overseas than in Korea. It was speculated that he was doing what he did best, thinking ahead of the time. But he suffered from a heart attack in 2014, so it is uncertain whether he will be able to resume his leadership. Even if he is fully recovered, KH and a few geniuses can't create Samsung's future alone. To identify new ventures or introduce creative solutions, Samsung must discover and develop new talent who will help them become first movers. Samsung's recent acquisitions of start-ups in Germany, Israel, the U.S. and the Netherlands are encouraging moves. To fully utilize these talents, Samsung will benefit from creating an organizational culture in which executives feel safe to take risks for strategic goals and employees feel free to disagree with their managers for innovation. Externally Samsung will have to involve customers and include partners for collaboration throughout the innovation process, while streamlining its structure to maximize creativity and to minimize control.

In 1996 KH demanded Samsung to make products with a soul. The world would love to see original innovative masterpieces made with Samsung's corporate soul. Such "distinctively Samsung" products will be possible only through awakening and nurturing the souls of all Samsung employees with humanity.

# A PUPIL: THE WINDOW
# TO AN AUTHENTIC SOUL

During the Song Dynasty in China, there was a great copy artist named Mibul, also known as "Dr. Calligraphy and Painting." He was exceptionally good at copying artworks, so artists themselves often couldn't distinguish his from theirs. Mibul also found great joy in testing collectors how well they knew their collections. He frequently borrowed artworks from collectors, painted them exactly like the originals, and gave his fake artworks to the owners, keeping the originals. He was able to amass over 1,000 masterpieces, because none of the collectors could tell the difference between the original and the fake.

But his fate was about to change when he borrowed a painting by an 8th Century artist named Daesoong from a collector. Daesoong was the foremost expert on painting cows then. As usual, Mibul copied it overnight and took his own work to the collector. Within a half day, the collector angrily marched into his house and accused him of fraud. Reluctantly admitting his guilt, Mibul asked the collector how he knew it.

"Look at the cow's pupil. It has a reflection of a shepherd boy leading a cow." As he was bringing the original of Daesoong's work to the owner, Mibul was awed one more time, "Oh my God, I see the cow reflected in the pupil of the shepherd as well."

## CHAPTER 81

# Overcome the NIH (Not Invented Here) Syndrome

Years ago, I co-facilitated worldwide cultural change management programs for 1,000 managers of a leading U.S. multinational company. The so-called "Not Invented Here (NIH) Syndrome" was cited as the biggest barrier to cultural change of the organization. The employees in Asia and Europe complained that U.S. company policies and practices were too U.S.-centric. When the people at Headquarters believed that all the great ideas must come from the HQ office, different voices and diverse perspectives were ignored and subsidiary employees were uninspired.

Having worked with numerous global *Fortune* 500 companies, I've found that most corporations tend to be headquarters-centric regardless of their national origin. French companies are likely to be French-centric, Chinese companies Chinese-centric and Korean companies Korean-centric. Despite their international operations, most important decisions are often made at corporate headquarters without consulting local leaders. In managing cultural differences, people seem to think that "we" are always better than "they."

As Samsung's non-Korean employees outnumber its Korean workforce, SEC requires its Korean employees to write emails in both Korean and English for better international communication. They are given the option to use an automatic translation service. But beyond using a common business language, global executives and employees must realize that the best solutions often involve diverse thoughts and approaches. Samsung must be proactive in seeking the opinions of locals in making key decisions.

One former Samsung U.S. employee said, "Nothing overt. Just the impression that Koreans do not trust anything the Americans tell them. Many would like to deal with Koreans exclusively. We get the impression that some Koreans think less of the Americans and possibly perceive them to be lazy." Another complained that any e-mail address without a Korean name was not taken seriously. Even when the "Samsung Way" was rolled out globally, some overseas employees perceived it to be overly headquarters-centric.

For Samsung to be a leader in a creative economy, Samsung must welcome NIH and embrace global diversity and inclusion more widely. When everyone's idea is valued equally, employees will be motivated to contribute to the company. In a speech on public policy, world-renown cellist Yo-Yo Ma summarized the edge effect for creativity and innovation:

> *"Where two ecosystems meet, there is the greatest diversity of life in addition to the greatest number of new life forms because of the influence that the two ecological communities have on each other."*

For Samsung to be a first mover, it must create the transition zone where people from diverse cultures can leverage the edge effect. In order to balance headquarters control with local autonomy, Samsung must actively develop local talent. While global employees exceeded 60% of SEC's workforce in 2012, its top 50 executives were all Korean. Fewer than 2% of Samsung executives were foreigners and very few of them had P&L (profit and loss) responsibilities. As of May 2014, SEC's top three leaders in the USA were also Korean expats, but the need for appointing local hires for top positions with decision-making power will get stronger as was the case with Korean subsidiaries of non-Korean multinationals. Lack of career path or a feeling of exclusion will prevent Samsung from recruiting and retaining the best global talent.

## CHAPTER 82

# Upgrade Leadership with a Global Mindset

As a global leadership coach, I have learned that cross-cultural skills are easier to teach than a global mindset. During the 2000s, a few Korean multinationals such as LG Electronics, Doosan Infracore and SK Group strategically hired foreign executives for their corporate headquarters leadership positions as a part of their globalization initiatives. LG Electronics, for a while, even adopted an English only policy at executive meetings at the Korean Headquarters. It was a few years before Rakuten, a Japanese web commerce firm, introduced "Englishnization" for business communication in 2010. The English only policy gave Korean executives and employees enormous stress. Instead of trying to speak in English, some chose to stay silent. Skeptics also questioned whether foreigners could bring any positive impact to them because of language and cultural barriers. However, their top management saw it as an investment: Korean executives working side-by-side with non-Korean leaders would improve their global mindset and cross-cultural competencies. Interestingly, Samsung has kept their headquarters leadership team with mainly Koreans, successfully creating global products and executing global marketing strategies so far.

KH has lived and studied in Japan and the U.S., and has traveled the world, so he appreciated global diversity and believed in the power of heterogeneous teams. Many Samsung senior leaders in Korea have also studied overseas or have taken expat assignments. Such experiences can improve cultural awareness and understanding, although overseas experience is not always a guarantee for cross-cultural competence. Some of them may be visionary and globally minded; however, other leaders, managers and employees at Samsung need to upgrade global leadership and communication competencies. The global mindset is more critical to Samsung's success than ever, as it seeks a new business model for innovation and growth through international mergers and acquisitions.

One American employee said, "I tried repeatedly to explain to Korean managers that U.S. workers work best when they understand the context—the 'why'—of a request or direction." Another employee wrote, "It is difficult to convince Korean colleagues of the value of advanced planning and strategy; Koreans tend to focus only on the very short-term objectives and thrive on 'just-in-time' action."

International managers at global corporations like Samsung will benefit from applying what I call "the seven pillars" of cultural intelligence: global literacy, mentality, identity, competency, technology, integrity and humanity. Global mentality is open-mindedness to different views, opinions, lifestyles, etc. Those who have it:

- Are relentlessly curious about other cultures
- Rethink their boundaries beyond a national border
- See the benefit of working with global diversity
- Check their assumptions about the world around them
- Shift their paradigms as necessary
- Acknowledge cultural differences and relativity
- Accept cross-cultural challenges and conflicts as natural.

One Korean Samsung expatriate manager in the U.S. told me that it took him one year to realize that if he thinks that an American's behavior is strange, the American would also perceive his Korean behavior as strange too. It takes discipline and hard work to develop cross-cultural intelligence. Chinese philosopher Confucius said:

- When you meet someone or see something, avoid preconceived notions.
- Don't say that things must be done only this way.
- Listen to other peoples' perspectives with respect. Don't try to impose your ideas upon others.
- Don't think that you are the only one who can do a particular job.

Such mindsets and attitudes will help Samsung men and women to be more adaptive and effective in working internationally after they leave Samsung. Many ex-Samsung managers who have joined other companies realize that the power and influence over their global colleagues and vendors they had at Samsung was not their own, but came from Samsung's organizational and purchasing power. So it is important for Samsung employees to develop "portable cultural competency" for their career management.

"*How shall I talk of the sea to the frog, if he has never left his pond?*

*How shall I talk of the frost to the bird of summer land if he has never left the land of its birth?*

*How shall I talk of life with the sage, if he is a prisoner of his doctrine?*"

— Chuang-Tzu

## CHAPTER 83

# Try Harder to Retain
# Global Talent

With a plan to open a new $300 million R&D center in Silicon Valley in 2015, Samsung has been reported to hire tech talent like crazy. In the epicenter of technology and innovation, Samsung is waging a war for talent against employers such as Apple, Google and Facebook. For Samsung to be an attractive employer in the U.S., Samsung will have to pay attention to company review websites like Glassdoor. Former and current employees have already posted their comments on Samsung's corporate culture, management style, pay, etc. Their comments are not quite favorable compared to Samsung's competition and may turn potential candidates away. If recruiting top talent is challenging, retaining them will be even harder.

In June 2013, I stayed at Ramada Hotel in Suwon, Samsung's Digital City. The only five-star hotel in the city was sold out due to Samsung's global employee training. It was great to see the diversity of trainees from all over the world. Their dynamic energy was filling the hotel and the city and I could feel the "edge effect" on learning and innovation. As I always do for my clients, I prayed that all of them would fulfill their dreams and potential at Samsung. I wanted them to stay with Samsung for a long time, although that may not be realistic. A Chinese executive of a U.S. multinational operating in China asked me whether Samsung would be a good company to work for. He said, "When recruiters call me, I am curious about Samsung, but I am afraid to take the risk because my former boss joined Samsung and didn't last a year. He was very good." In April 2014, CNET reported that at least five high-ranking executives from Samsung Telecommunications America (STA), Samsung's U.S. mobile business, had either left the company or given their notice. That could be interpreted as a sign that Samsung employees are sought after in the job market. Still one cannot deny that there are cross-cultural challenges to be resolved. What are some of the challenges that non-Koreans face in working for a Korean company? Below is a sampling of the issues that Americans have identified:

- Communication barriers
- Unclear direction
- Koreans' lack of understanding (or unwillingness to follow) local business practices
- Lack of empowerment
- Powerful dispatchers (Korean expats on assignment)
- Lack of information sharing and feedback
- Lack of work-life balance due to a demanding schedule
- Not sharing the big picture
- Not seeking or utilizing local input
- Korean dispatchers doing subordinates' work (instead of delegating or developing)

These are very similar to the barriers encountered by Americans who worked for Japanese companies in the 1980s or 1990s. Having worked with Korean expatriates, I can easily guess how some of them will respond to these comments: Americans seem to consider their personal life more important than work and Americans don't work on evenings or weekends even if work needs to be done. To prevent Korean managers from overgeneralizing American workers, I tell them that many Americans log in to their laptops and tablets during evenings and weekends, finishing up their work; those who may leave work early to pick up children or coach their children's sports teams frequently work again after spending their family time in the evening.

Hiring the right person with a cultural fit is the key to any multinational's global talent management. Samsung must overcome the perception that it prefers "yes men" for easy control in its overseas operations. "I just do what I am told to do," answered a manager when I asked about the secret of her longevity at a Samsung Asia-Pacific subsidiary with a high turnover rate. Mark Newman, an analyst who worked for Samsung for six years, was quoted in *BusinessWeek*, "If you can't follow a specific directive, you can't stay at the firm."

How can Samsung accomplish innovation without valuing diversity? To benefit from the diversity of thoughts, Samsung must welcome different voices and opinions across the globe. Its leaders and managers need to encourage and listen to straightforward feedback from global employees as KH did with Japanese advisors. Cross-cultural

192

challenges are common and natural for global teams. Once they overcome them, they tend to be much more productive. The following ideas may be helpful:

- Develop strategies that will help employees discover their own cultural tendencies, learn from and adapt to each other.
- Accept the cultural assumptions and expectations of others as valid in their countries and cultures.
- Continue to adopt new ways of thinking and working—both/and, rather than either your way or my way.

## CHAPTER 84

# Work Smart, Play Smart

*"Someday everybody will work for themselves. They will come to work to enjoy themselves."*

— Soichiro Honda, Founder of Honda

For Korean college graduates, SEC has been voted as the #1 company to work for. Why is it so popular? The high salary is certainly attractive. And there's prestige attached to the Samsung name. A single Korean guy who works at Samsung can impress a potential bride and his in-laws to be.

Unfortunately, Samsung's corporate culture is rarely mentioned as a compelling reason to work there. Samsung has been running a "Great Place to Work For" campaign, but is known for an extremely competitive and high-stress environment. Despite its "Work Smart" campaign, there is a perception of having no work-life balance. In 2014, SEC got 3.5 out of 5 (highest) on Job Planet, a Korean version of Glassdoor on which former and current employees evaluate their employers and post their experience. SEC's score was lower than Hyundai Motors, POSCO and LG Chemicals. A reporter summarized the postings for SEC: "Great for money and recognition, but not recommended for work-life balance." Some even say that there are "Samsung widows," because "Samsung men" are often expected to be "on call" in the evening and on weekends, unless they are detached from career advancement.

Reportedly KH got the idea of 7:00 AM to 4 :00 PM work hours for Samsung employees when he took a Samsung employee commuter bus to a factory several years before he introduced it with New Management 1.0 in 1993. Since his face was partially covered with a big hat, nobody noticed him. However, he must have seen the tired look on the faces of employees who were going to work for another long day. He was convinced that the quality of Samsung products would go up with improved quality of life of employees. Thus, he encouraged employees to work efficiently during work hours and to enjoy the rest. In March 2014, I was in Suzhou, China. I saw charter buses waiting at my hotel to take Samsung employees to factories. The commuters were Korean employees on business trips from Korea. I wondered whether KH would have noticed anything different on their faces, compared to the first time he took a Samsung commuter bus more than 20 years ago. Although the pressure may vary depending on the industry, company, function and production schedule of each affiliate, Samsung is still perceived as a very demanding place with long hours with no play.

A recent Korean on-line posting compared the different types of talent doing well at various Korean corporations. The advice for Samsung employees: "Don't stand out. Samsung is run by the top 1% of its employee base—elite leaders—and the rest (99%) operate like robots." Working with other non-Korean multinationals, I've heard similar complaints from their employees around the world, "I feel like a cog in the wheel." Such comments from employees of a large conglomerate like SEC are not surprising, but Samsung must address those perceptions in order to attract more talent with *kki*, which is loosely translated as an "independent and creative spirit."

If Samsung wants to compete with Google and other innovative companies of the world for the best talent, they need to create a "cool" environment that inspires them. Especially if Samsung wants to hire "geniuses," Samsung will need to create an environment to spark divergent thinking. Across the globe, employees want to work with positive people and be treated with respect in addition to being challenged and learning new knowledge and skills. In a Korean job market with overeducated applicants due to a strong zeal for education, young Koreans may have to compete for each Samsung spot. However, many don't have the same hungry spirit and dedication to employers that older Koreans used to show after the Korean War. Besides, global employees often have more choices for their employer.

Samsung seems to be making some progress on the global recruiting front. It thrived during and after the recession of 2008. One executive of a U.S. high-tech R&D center told me, "I've lost many of my employees to Samsung. Engineers are excited to work on the newest gadgets and are happy to develop cutting edge products. At Samsung, they seem to be given that opportunity."

Samsung must still continue to inspire new talent in order to recruit and retain them even in a good economy, inside and outside of Korea. As KH stated, leaders should transform their leadership style from "follow me" to "after you," by first "giving employees DIY (Do It Yourself) opportunities" with accountability.

"Cherish Your Inner Voice and Your Inner Feelings"—this inscription is placed outdoors on a Samsung campus. Samsung must become a place for employees to make those words come to life.

> *"Don't worry about checking-in at work. It doesn't matter wherever you work—at home or work—as long as you THINK. It doesn't have to be done at the company. It's OK to play for six months after working relentlessly for six months...But make sure that you play smart."*
> — KH Lee, June 1993

## CHAPTER 85

# Loosen Control

Confucius said in *The Analects*:

> *"If you govern by regulations and keep them in order for punishment, the people will avoid trouble but have no sense of shame. If you govern them by moral influence, and keep them in order by a code of manners, they will have a sense of shame and will come to you of their own accord."*

Several years ago, my son and I were walking on a beach in South Beach, Florida. A Korean boy of my son's age was playing alone in the sand. Soon the boys were swimming together and his mother joined us. I found out that her husband had just completed his MBA in the USA, and the family wanted to take a short break before returning to Korea. He was one of several Samsung employees who were given an opportunity to study abroad with a company sponsorship. "Please don't tell any Samsung people that you met us here," the mother requested. "No one at the company knows about this. My husband's boss expected him to return to work after the last day of school."

It is not just middle-level managers who worry about being "watched" at Samsung. Executives don't also seem to feel free about their personal activities when they are away from the office. They are mindful of their reputation even in private gatherings. In fact, some executives said that their chauffeurs and secretaries were like bosses because they knew their whereabouts. Even overseas, senior Korean leaders seem to be aware of the eyes of "Corporate Headquarters." While American expat executives and their spouses are actively involved in local communities in their host countries, Samsung expatriate leaders usually keep a low profile and do not seek visibility through public appearances. While their active participation in civic or business organizations in host countries would enhance their cultural competence and Samsung's corporate image, many tend to avoid any attention that might negatively affect their career back home.

Here is another example of control. A U.S. Samsung sales manager said that he had been asked to submit a picture of the venue and attendees along with receipts for an expense report for dinner with customers. Trust is certainly earned over time, so there may be a reason for such a request. However, do all these rules for control improve employees' honesty or integrity? They must have played a part in Samsung's reputation as a relatively "clean" organization. But there is a Chinese saying, "Too much is as bad as too little ( 過猶不及 )." Samsung must ask whether there are too many rules and regulations for employees that are not conducive to promoting ethics and integrity.

A Korean-American engineer with a Ph.D. shared his experience with a Samsung global recruiter. After talking with his friends and family, he decided not to pursue an opportunity at Samsung. But the recruiter requested that he travel for a face-to-face interview with a hiring executive. The candidate said that he didn't want to waste any time for both parties because he wasn't planning to join Samsung, but the recruiter insisted on his travel. "We are measured by the people who come to interviews," the recruiter pleaded. "Please consider my position too." Appealing to a humanistic side of a person is very Korean, and it is possible that the recruiter really believed that a face-to-face interview would lead to a change of heart.

One Korean executive who has done business with both Samsung and Hyundai said, "I was so impressed with Hyundai employees' love for their company and I haven't seen such affection for the company at Samsung." Hyundai's founder, Joo-Young Jeong, once recollected about his teen years as a laborer at a construction site, "When the sun rose in the morning, my heart was beating fast with excitement for the joy of working." He was able to create the same passion and dedication from Hyundai employees through charisma and camaraderie, not through control. Not surprisingly, Hyundai men are often considered more warm-hearted and humanistic than Samsung men.

KH asked Samsung leaders several times, "Samsung is ranked # 1 in many product categories. But have we ever changed the rules of the game [in any industry]?" As he asserted, "An organization without autonomy is dead." It's time for Samsung to change the rules of the game, rather than add more rules for control. Balanced control will not only increase autonomy and accountability in management, but also enhance a sense of humanity emphasized in the Samsung Constitution.

## CHAPTER 86

# Pursue Co-Prosperity
# with Partners

*[The relationships between] large corporations and small-to-medium*
*companies are similar to those of married couples.*

— KH Lee

A U.S. start-up company was very excited about getting more funding from investors. The CEO told me that the condition for additional funding was to win a Samsung account within six months. He travelled to Korea frequently, hired local agents and built relationships with Samsung customers. His hard work paid off. He finally won the business. A couple of months later, I asked him how his company was doing. He said, "Customers are happy, but we are hurting. The price is so low."

Many Korean suppliers say similar things: Samsung squeezes them so much, even when Samsung announces record profits. So there is a saying among Samsung suppliers, "You don't make much profit from doing business with Samsung, but you won't go bankrupt." Despite the prestige and volume, some say that it's not much fun to be a Samsung supplier.

With the Korean government's encouragement, Samsung has been working on supplier partnership programs for co-prosperity. Samsung announced that it would share certain intellectual property with small-to-medium size Korean companies. SEC also announced its plan to give special incentives to 4,000 subcontractors who work at their plants in Ki-Heung, Hwa-Sung and Gyeonggi-do from 2014. Depending on their company's rating, they will receive about $1,500 to $5,000 per person.

In addition, Samsung has introduced some unique, innovative programs for partners. For example, Samsung provided educational programs for "the 2nd generation of Samsung partner companies." The children of the owners were hired by Samsung for a one-year period to experience Samsung and to learn its philosophy and culture. Interestingly, during the good days of Panasonic, its suppliers felt the vision and management philosophy of its founder Konosuke Matsushita and became one with Panasonic. KH had such a vision. Once in a luncheon with Samsung suppliers, KH asked one of them:

- What kind of car do you drive?
- Where do you park?
- Are you getting access to our R&D centers (even when other Samsung enterprise leaders don't have it)?

He meant that Samsung suppliers should be able to afford luxury cars and have access to good parking spaces and R&D centers. These are great goals; however, one of the most fundamental rules of engagement should be to treat partners with dignity and respect. A former partner of a top U.S. management consulting company said that it is difficult to find consultants who want to be on Samsung projects because of its reputation: Samsung will treat them disrespectfully. Other suppliers also concur that Samsung hurts themselves with an overly authoritarian attitude and draconian behaviors toward suppliers.

Furthermore, Samsung's information control makes it very difficult for many vendors to provide the most effective solutions. Samsung account managers of multinationals deplore that "EVERYTHING is confidential at Samsung, so we are not given the information to solve their problems in a timely manner or correctly." IP protection is absolutely critical to all global companies, but Samsung will achieve better results through balanced and prudent information management. Henry Chesbrough, professor of University of Berkeley Haas School of Business and author of *Open Innovation*, wrote:

> *"Companies can no longer keep their own innovations secret unto themselves; ... the key to success is creating, in effect, an open platform around your innovations so your customers, your employees and even your competitors can build upon it, because only by that building will you create an ongoing, evolving community of users, doers and creators."*

KH also said, "Information is like joy which is multiplied when it is shared with others. The value of information increases only when it is distributed to others." Samsung's open communication and collaboration with partners will contribute to co-learning and innovation.

As a global corporation, Samsung must eliminate the notion that suppliers should or would "do as we say," even if Korean suppliers have done so for many years. If Samsung treats its suppliers with trust and respect, and shares the necessary information for them to do a good job, Samsung will gain more respect and become true partners with the world's best-in-class suppliers. Only then will Samsung partners also care about Samsung's prosperity and be loyal to Samsung.

## CHAPTER 87

# Do the Right Thing

In 2010, KH returned to Samsung as CEO after two years of absence in the wake of Samsung's financial scandal. It is a common Korean practice for a condemned leader to go on a self-imposed "exile" for public redemption and private reflection. So KH didn't make any public appearances for those two years. He never had to serve his jail term because he received a Presidential pardon.

Several months after the pardon, the book *Justice: What is the Right Thing to Do?* by Harvard Professor Michael Sandel became a bestseller in Korea. Did the pardon of KH spark Koreans' interest in the topic of justice? The bestselling book's Korean title, *What Is Justice?* reflected the Korean psyche of that time. "Winning is justice or justice is winning (at all costs)," some complained. Others argued that justice alone can't "feed the people" (many Korean expressions have eating/food-related terms) and were willing to accept a compromise of principles over profit.

SEC has provided much livelihood to Koreans, contributing to 15% -17% of Korea's annual GDP. The entire Samsung group's contribution has been over 29% of Korea's GDP. Therefore, KH's leadership has been critical not only to Samsung, but also to Korea. Were Koreans looking for answers for justice from Sandel's book? If so, Koreans weren't the only Asians with a curiosity about justice. Thomas Friedman, a Pulitzer Prize winning *New York Times* writer, wrote that Sandel had received rock star treatment in other East Asian countries.

Traditionally in Korea, there were four classes: scholar, farmer, craftsman and merchant in descending order. Why were farmers above merchants? They were perceived to be hard-working and more honest than merchants who might have to manipulate the market to gain profit. Thus, in Asia "the way of merchants" was touted to set the examples of ethical businessmen who put principles over profit. More recently a popular Korean TV series entitled *The Way of Merchants* showed businessmen the right path to prosperity with a key message, "Wealth is like water, which cannot be monopolized."

Before trying to win the respect of global citizens, Samsung needs to earn the trust and respect of its fellow citizens in Korea first. In an article entiled "Samsung's War at Home," Cam Simpson of *Bloomberg Businessweek* (April 10, 2014) examined the cases of former Samsung factory workers who had died of leukemia or suffered from other blood-related cancers. Korean activists and their families believe that the workers were exposed to toxic chemicals, but Samsung denied any corelation between their illness and the factory environment. Interestingly about a month after the report, Samsung Vice Chairman Oh-Hyun Kwon apologized to sickened former employees and promised compensation for them and their families. Some interpreted it as a reflection of KH's will to resolve this issue before his son JY takes over Samsung, so that he can start his leadership role with a clean slate.

While these cases are still unresolved, if Samsung wants to be a world-class company, it must strive to become a role model of good capitalism and ethical entrepreneurship. Occupational safety of Samsung employees and partners should be guaranteed. Co-prosperity is one of Samsung's core values and now it is time to show it through its actions.

As Iwakuni Tesundo, a former investment banker for Merrill Lynch and former mayor of Izumo City in Japan, suggested in an interview with a Korean newspaper *Maeil Economic Daily*: "Samsung will become a great company if Samsung can add one more 'S' for "Share" in addition to its existing 4S's (Study, Service, Sense and Speed). Sharing for Samsung should mean more than charity or good will gestures. Samsung has great opportunities to work with Korean start-ups or small businesses with fewer resources. Samsung must collaborate with them instead of competing with them. Samsung needs to contribute to creating and maintaining a viable ecosystem for young and creative entrepreneurs in Korea, instead of snatching them away for Samsung.

Bill Gates, Founder of Microsoft, quoted his mother's last wish for him and his wife in his 2007 Commencement Address at Harvard University:

> *"From those to whom much is given, much is expected"*
> — Luke 12:48

It's worthwhile for Samsung leaders to contemplate on the founder's question when they have a choice to do good vs. evil. They can also be inspired by Google's corporate slogan "Don't be evil."

## BC's QUESTION ON DEATHBED

A few years ago, a Korean Catholic priest posted 24 questions BC had asked in a memo sent to another priest one month before his death. BC didn't practice any religion in his life, but on his deathbed, he queried the priest on spiritual matters such as God, religion and soul. His 16th question to the priest was particularly intriguing: "According to the Bible, it is easier for a camel to go through the eye of a needle, than for a rich man to enter the kingdom of God. Does it mean that the rich are evil people?" BC never got to hear the priest's answers because he had died before a meeting was rescheduled.

## CHAPTER 88

# Inspire the World with Humility and Grace

*"Without sufficient strength of our soul, we can easily become a slave to our own talents."*

— Kazuo Inamori

"Forget the past successes and let's start over," said KH in his 2013 New Year's speech for Samsung employees.

While Samsung has not been ostentatiously celebrating its record profits quarter after quarter, many people believe that Samsung is too arrogant. It may be just a perception, but Samsung will further enhance its global image by practicing humility, which is one of the greatest Asian virtues. When we grew up in Korea, we were told to be like rice plants; as they mature, they lower their heads. Samsung has achieved great success, but they have to watch out for the price of success, so that they won't fall into the trap of overconfidence. KH also expressed his concern about Samsung people's "self-satisfaction" that might lead to their complacency and downfall.

The global presence of Samsung TVs, phones and appliances is not the same as Samsung's universal power and influence. It is certainly not the sign of Samsung's contribution to humanity. Samsung's greatness will not be achieved when it reaches the $400 billion revenue mark or hires the largest number of employees. How can Samsung become great? "Treat the people you do business with as if they are a part of your family," said the founder of Panasonic. How inspiring it would be if Samsung employees, partners and customers feel warmth, generosity and sincerity in their interaction with Samsung.

The most basic consideration will be for the well-being of fellow citizens. Mr. Soichiro Honda, founder of the Honda Motor Company, directed in his will not to hold a company-wide funeral service, which was commonly given to founders and leaders of large corporations. He was concerned that it would cause traffic jams and inconvenience commuters. "Such behavior should be prohibited for an auto company," said Mr. Honda. This may look like a small gesture from a corporate giant, but it has a huge impact on people and a company's image. If Samsung men and women demonstrate such humility and respect, not only in business transactions but also in their personal conduct, they will wow the citizens of the world.

*Jūnzǐ* (great man) is the Confucian ideal of a perfect human being. He is mature, magnanimous, respectful and helpful towards others. A *jūnzǐ* will be an ideal business leader because he is trustworthy, has good etiquette, and listens humbly. A Samsung *jūnzǐ* will revere all people regardless of their nationality, color, race and creed, and treat them as a part of their family.

Confucius reportedly had a great influence on BC, the founder of Samsung. If every Samsung executive and employee strives to become a *jūnzǐ*, Samsung can become one of the world's most inspiring companies in history, bringing harmony and prosperity to the world. Only then will the founder's vision of Samsung lasting for 300 years (or even 1,000 years) be worthwhile and all the people who have worked at Samsung would be able to proudly say: "I have fulfilled my professional life with meaning." Samsung's ultimate vision should be to build a company with a soul and employees with prospering souls. Then innovative products with a soul will naturally follow.

# Epilogue

On a Sunday evening in late July 2013, I took a taxi from the Frankfurt Central Station to the birthplace of Samsung's "cultural revolution," the Kempinski Hotel Gravenbruch. I had a business trip to Germany and wouldn't miss an opportunity to see where KH made the famous "Frankfurt Declaration." One week before, I completed my final edits to this book and was eager to experience the energy and feelings KH and his lieutenants might have felt at the hotel in 1993. So I made a two-night reservation at the hotel.

The hotel, a former hunting lodge, was going through a major renovation, but I tried to imagine its serenity 20 years ago. Surrounded by forests and parks, it had a private lake, a tennis court, swimming pools, sunbathing areas and a sauna. I thought that most Koreans would have loved the sauna there, although the co-ed facility might have been a culture shock to them. It is very unlikely that any of Samsung's executives would have used it during their stay. Given the serious nature of the meetings in which they were told to "Change everything except your wife and children," no "Samsung men" would have dared to roam around the property to relax. Two hotel employees who had met them confirmed that the attendees were all about work.

A manager showed me the ballroom where the historical meetings were held for several weeks. It was also under renovation, but I visualized KH on the podium and the crowd in the room. For Samsung, this ballroom was a historical place. *BusinessWeek* reported that Samsung had brought all the furnishings, including the chairs, tablecloth, and a painting from the meeting room to exactly recreate the "Frankfurt Room" at the Human Resources Development Center in Yongin, Korea. In 2012, Samsung also sent its new hire "expedition" team to this "holy place" for a TV documentary on "The New Management Roads" (like the Silk Road) in celebration of the 20th anniversary of New Management.

The Presidential Suite (Rm. 312) was where KH had stayed. With a view of a lake, it had a library in the loft, Swarovski crystal chandeliers, and Samsung Smart TVs—a vivid reminder of Samsung's revolution at the hotel. In the living room there was a 75-inch Samsung TV and in the formal meeting/dining room was another 60-inch Samsung Smart TV that could be used for presentations. Would the five-star hotel have had Samsung TVs in guest rooms, much less in its presidential suite 20 years ago? A concierge admitted that the hotel staff didn't know much about Samsung then. Walking around the suite, I wondered what KH would have thought during his stay. He might not have slept much. He talked about his insomnia in the past due to his fear of Samsung's collapse. Reportedly, on the way to Frankfurt in 1993, he was up for 30 hours straight, reading the "Fukuda report" and discussing solutions with his staff.

Most Samsung guests stayed in the rooms around the suite. Breakfast had to be delivered for some because they were up and working before the hotel restaurants were open. Samsung also brought its own cook (probably for KH).

I asked myself, "Where would the Samsung men be now?" A Samsung executive told me, "The owner of a Korean conglomerate (like Samsung) runs a marathon, but professional managers run long distances and employees run short-distances or even relays." The owner needs to know how to bring the best out of them while they are running with him, because very few professional managers are likely to finish a marathon with him. Many of the people whom KH led 20 years ago are no longer with Samsung, but KH, the myterious founder's son, is still running with some long distance runners and a few new short distance runners. Dominated by his charisma, Samsung has distinctive characteristics in Korea, yet outside of Korea, Samsung seems to be another giant global company without a soul. That must have been a concern for KH who demanded that Samsung employees make products with a soul, especially when he is heading to the finish line and preparing his son to run a new marathon.

Since KH was keen on reading the times through frequent travels, books and discussions, he often saw the megatrends in the global economic landscape earlier than others. KH didn't return to the Frankfurt hotel in 2013, but I saw one clear sign of change in the global economy—Chinese tourists. In the 1990s, most Asian tourists traveling in Europe were Japanese. During the 2000s, Korean tourists joined them, and now the world travel industry is getting ready for Chinese tourists with a Mandarin-speaking sales force and Chinese cuisine. Here comes a thought that might keep KH or JY up at night: 20 years from now (or even in 5 to 10 years), the Chinese tourists may see 4D TVs made by a Chinese innovator in their hotel rooms across the globe.

In July 2013, KH returned to Korea from another long strategic thinking session in Europe and Japan. The last week of July and the first week of August are known as an official holiday period for Samsung Group presidents, but KH showed up at work for two consecutive weeks upon his return. Usually he worked at his home office, so his presence at the Headquarters office got Korean media attention and sent his lieutenants and employees a strong message: It was a very critical period for Samsung. *TV Chosun* reported that the Vice Chairman Gee-Sung Choi was summoned for an "emergency meeting" during his vacation and other Samsung presidents were spending their vacation near Seoul, just in case.

The genius of KH was that he was able to execute the mega changes of a giant corporation. Having worked on change management projects, I am aware of numerous change initiatives that failed. Now the question is whether KH or his successor can execute another effective change management through "Mach Management" envisioned by KH. Who will take Samsung to the next level? The context is very different now. Unlike 1993, Samsung is no longer a Korean company selling overseas. Back then, most overseas employees didn't know much about the Frankfurt Declaration nor had they adopted the language of Samsung. If the New Management 1.0 were of Koreans, by Koreans and for Koreans, New Management for Samsung 3.0 must be executed on a global scale.

As of 2013, SEC's foreign employee population exceeded 60%. A change initiative designed by one Chairman at the Headquarters will no longer be effective for a global giant. Samsung has to include global talent in the change management process and share their vision with the global workforce. There is a long road ahead of Samsung, but I'm looking forward to being inspired by Samsung 3.0., which could lead to Samsung's 3rd Start–Up, igniting the challenging and entrepreneurial spirit of all employees around the world. As KH suggested in his essay, Samsung may need to go back to basics for its renewal.

My original intent for writing this book was to help Samsung employees, competitors and partners learn from its best practices and Asian wisdom. However, writing this book gave me an opportunity to reflect on my own cultural revolution. I asked myself, "If I were to change everything except for my spouse and child, how would I be transformed?" Samsung's change has a message for everyone who wants to embrace self-renewal and personal transformation in the age of uncertainty. From our daily language to work habits, we can incorporate positive Samsung ways into our lives to execute a revolution within and make our lives a masterpiece. I thank you for starting the journey with me.

# Acknowledgements

I'd like to thank the following people who have made this book's publication possible:

My valued clients: Thank you for encouraging me to write this book. I have learned a lot from your cross-cultural curiosity, insight and wisdom.

Byung-Chull (BC) Lee and Kun-Hee (KH) Lee: Your vision and leadership was truly inspiring. Your eyes and ears for talent, technology and timing have been critical to Samsung's success. Thank you for showing us the road to possibilities, especially for those in underdeveloped or developing countries.

Samsung employees: Without your hard work and dedication, the world would not have known Samsung or have been much interested in Korea.

Korean authors who have written books on Samsung in Korean. Thank you for sharing your findings and opinions as journalists, former employees, and professionals. Thanks to your contribution to the growing body of research on Samsung through your publications, international readers will finally get to learn about some of your works and better understand Samsung and Korea.

All the journalists who have contributed to Samsung-related articles for major newspapers and magazines, including Korea's *Chosun Daily*, *Maeil Economic Daily*, *The New York Times*, *The Financial Times*, *The Wall Street Journal*, *Forbes*, *Business Week*, *Fortune* and *Fast Company*.

Edward Iwata, author of *Fusion Entrepreneurship* and *A Billionaire's Gift*. Thank you for your valuable comments after reading the first draft. This book has benefited from your writing talent and keen editorial eyes.

Lincoln Valdez, thank you for your tireless support in the editing process.

Last, but not least, Edward C. Valdez, my partner and the best friend: Your collaboration has made this project much more fun and exciting. Your contribution has tremendously improved the quality of the book. I will be forever grateful to your support during many late night hours and weekends.

# Bibliography

**Books in Korean**

Bae, Duk-Sang. *Inside Samsung*, Midas Boos, 2012.

Cho, Young-Hwan. *Why CEOs from Samsung Are Strong*, BookOcean, 2012.

Hong, Ha-Sang. *Byung-chull Lee vs. Joo-Young Jeong*, Han-kook Kyung-jae Shin-moon, 2001.

Hong, Ha-Sang. *Osaka Merchants*, Hyo-hyung Chool-pan, 2008.

Jeon, Ok-Pyo. *Winning Habits*, Sam and Parkers, 2007.

Jeon, Yong-Wuk and Hahn, Jeong-ho. *The Road to the World Class Company* (Samsung's Growth and Change), Gimmyoung Publisher, 1994.

Joong-Ang Ilbo Economy Dept. II. *Movers and Shakers of the Korean Industry*, Joong-ang Ilbo, 1996.

Kang, Jin-Koo. *Samsung Electronics: Myth and the Secrets,* Ko-ryo-won, 1996.

Kim, Byung-Wan. *Smart War: Why Samsung in the End?* Brainstore, 2013.

Kim, Hae-Shik. *I Am a Samsung Man*, Kook-il Media, 2011.

Kim, Yong-Cheol. *Think Samsung*, Sa-hoe-pyung-ron, 2010.

Kim, Yoo-Jin. *Samsung and China*, Dong-yang-moon-ko, 2005.

Kim, Sung-Hong and Woo, In-Ho. *Kun-hee Lee's Ten-year Revolution*, Gimm-young-sa, 2003.

Konotsuke, Matsushita. *The Mindset for Entrepreneurship*, Cheong-lim Chul-pan, 2007.

Koo, Bon-Hyung. *Seek from People*, Eul-yoo-moon-wha-sa, 2007.

Lee, Chae-Yoon. *Samsung Electronics 3.0 Story,* Book Ocean, 2011.

Lee, Chae-Yoon. *Manage like Samsung*, Yeol-mae Chul-pan-sa, 2004.

Lee, Chang-Woo. *Learn from Byung-Chull Lee Again*, Seoul Moon-wha-sa, 2003.

Lee, Jong-Gon. *Samsung Spirit, Hyundai Spirit*, Jae-sam-moon-hak-sa, 1995.

Lee, Kun-Hee. *Kun-Hee Lee Essays*. Dong-a Ilbo, 1997.

Park, Sang-Ha. *Mong-Koo Chung Who Wins, Kun-Hee Lee Who Doesn't Lose*, Pen House, 2012.

Park, Won-Bae and Ahn, Young Bae. *Learn from Enemies: Hyundai-Samsung Stealing from Each Other*, Cheong-maek, 1994.

Shin, Yong-In. *Samsung vs. Intel,* Random House Korea, 2009.

Sung, Hwa-Yong. *2015: Jae Yong Lee's Samsung*, Monthly Chosun, 2005.


**Books in English**

Byham, William. *Shogun Management*, HarperBusiness, 1993.

Issacson, Walter. *Steve Jobs*, Simon & Schuster, 2011.

Kim, Eun Y. *Global Intelligence: Seven Pillars for Global Leaders*, CEO International, 2001.

Kim, Eun Y. *The Yin and Yang of American Culture: A Paradox*, Intercultural Press, 2001.

Kim, Eun-Young. *A Cross-cultural Reference of Business Practices in a New Korea*, Prager, 1996.

March, James. *Working for a Japanese Company*, Kodansha International, 1996.

Morita, Akio. *Made in Japan*, Signet, 1988.

Rosen, Robert. *Global Literacies*, Simon & Schuster, 2000.

Slater, Robert. *The GE Way Fieldbook*, McGraw-Hill, 2000.

Trompenaars, Fons. *Riding the Waves of Culture: Understanding Diversity in Global Business*, Irwin, 1997.

Wing, R. L. *The Tao of Power: Lao-Tzu's Classic Guide to Leadership, Influence and Excellence*, Double Day & Co., 1986.

Wylie, Arthur. *Confucius and Lao-Tzu: The Analects of Confucius and Tao-Te-Ching*, Barnes & Noble, 2005.


## On-line Tools and Resources

*Cultural Detective South Korea* by Kim, Eun Y., Park, Joon-hyung, and Saphiere, Dianne H.
*American Society of Training and Development (ASTD) 2012 State of the Industry Report:* Organizations Continue to Invest in Workplace Learning


## Newspapers and Magazines

*Chosun Daily* (www.chosun.com)
*Maeil Economic Daily*
*The Financial Times*
*The Wall Street Journal*
*The New York Times*
*Business Chosun*
*Harvard Business Review*
*Forbes*
*Fortune*
*Bloomberg Businessweek*
*Fast Company*


## Samsung Group and Electronics Websites and Reports

*Samsung Corporate Website with Samsung Group vision and philosophy*
*Samsung Electronics Sustainability Report 2012*

# About the Authors

Dr. Eun Y. Kim is President of CEO International, a global leadership consulting firm. With a B.A. from Seoul National University, Korea and a Ph.D. from the University of Texas at Austin, Dr. Kim has worked in the U.S., Asia and Europe as a management consultant and executive coach and has taught around the globe. As an expert in global leadership, teamwork, executive presence and intercultural communication, she has worked with numerous Samsung entities, including semiconductors, R&D, telecommunication, engineering and construction, etc. A sampling of Dr. Kim's clients includes: Applied Materials, Aramco, Cisco, Dell, Deloitte, Freescale, IBM, LG, Marvell, Motorola, NPD, Oracle, Qualcomm, RealNetworks, Samsung, SanDisk, Sematech, SK Hynix, STMicroelectronics, Texas Instruments, Verizon, etc.

Dr. Kim has written nine books/guides and co-authored an on-line culture learning tool: *Cultural Detectives USA* and *South Korea.*

Edward Valdez is an executive of Learning List, an education solutions start-up. With over 25 years of experience in the high tech industry, he was an executive sponsor of Samsung at Sun Microsystems (now Oracle) and served as President of Parrot USA, a French wireless company. Prior to that, Ed held managerial positions at Motorola and IBM. As a contributor to *Technorati* and other media, Ed tracks mobile tech trends and the forces behind them with cultural insights. With a BSEE from MIT and an MBA from UT Austin, he also serves on the Board of Advisors for SXSWedu.

# Also by Eun Y. Kim, Ph.D.

*Seven UPs: A Guide to the
Good Life for Boomers and Gen-Xers*

*The Yin and Yang of
American Culture: A Paradox*

*Global Intelligence: Seven Pillars
for New Global Leaders*

*New Hispanics:
The New Image for New Leaders*

*Image-making* (Korean only*)*

*Managing Self for Success and Significance*

*A Cross-Cultural Reference of
Business Practices in a New Korea*